WAITING FOR **GREATNESS**

Memories & Musings of a Sports Television Cameraman

JOHN P. MARTIN

Cover designer: Tony Saia
Cover photo: Denise Hein
Formatting: Christine Borgford, Type A Formatting

TABLE OF CONTENTS

PREFACE

THE CONCEPT FOR this book has been taking shape for many years. I attempted on many cross-country flights to write it but could never seem to stay sober enough! Focus issues. I must first thank my wife, Adrienne, for supporting me the entire time I worked in television. There were many days, nights and weeks that I was not around as she held down the fort with our two daughters. She was and still is a true superstar! As are our kids Kaia and Gabby. I love you all so very much. I must also thank Jimmy Dunn and his bestseller, Funny Ball, for the inspiration for the format of this book. No chapter is too short, no thought or story is unworthy!

This was a very challenging book to write, as I was very careful to not name names in certain places to protect the guilty or the innocent as hard as that may have been. All stories are true and factual as well as my memory serves.

I was fortunate enough to enjoy a nineteen year career working in sports television in the Boston market. I worked as a videographer for a regional sports network (NESN) and traveled with two of the pro teams and worked with many talented individuals. There were lots of long nights and many times away from home and spending it with some of these people made it all the better. It was the greatest job I ever had.

I could not have been luckier than to have worked within the time period I did in regards to Boston sports teams winning championships! Think about it. The Patriots in '01, '03, '04, '14 and '16, the Celtics in '08, the Bruins '11 in and of course the Red Sox in '04, '07 and '13. Certainly, an unprecedented run by the local teams that may never be challenged.

A lot has changed technically in the close to twenty years I worked in the business, the biggest being the arrival of HD and the move from a 4 x 3 presentation to 16 x 9 and now 4K. The cameras themselves have also changed quite a bit, being smaller and more menu driven. That's all well and good but I've always said a few things throughout my career—'it's the fiddler not the fiddle and always use a tripod when possible.' In regards to the fiddler I mean it doesn't matter how new or how many 'bells 'n whistles' driven the equipment may be—it's always in the hands of a human being, a.k.a. 'the fiddler.' A great camera operator can make any camera sing!

As I've always told young camera operators and BryGuy, use a tripod as much as possible as it always makes a difference for a nice level bounceless shot. I've seen many young camera guys choke the heck out of their camera, which inevitably creates unnecessary shakiness. Man up and carry your tripod with you. And don't ever forget the 3 H's—soft hands, clear head and open heart!

Flat out effort to me is a huge component of what makes up a quality photographer. I never considered myself to be the best photographer out there but I sure made up for it in effort. That can go a long way. As Mike Narracci, famed director of Red Sox baseball, would often say 'just give me your best effort—we all have good days and bad days but you can never replace effort.' Well said, Papi.

The following pages contain a collection of memories and musings that hopefully you'll find entertaining. I couldn't tell all the stories here and you may be holding this future bestseller wondering why your story's not here. Well, tough cookies!

I was unexpectedly sent into retirement in October 2016 and always maintained throughout my career I would someday write a book.

Author Christopher Hitchens once said, "Everyone has a book in them, but in most cases, that's where it should stay."

Well, too bad!

Here is mine.

Enjoy!

FOREWORD

HE COULD'VE ASKED Pedro Martinez to write this. And Pedro, being the thoughtful person he is, probably would have. Definitely would have sold a few more books. But, my friend John Martin is too real for that. And I couldn't be more honored.

John has many life-long friends. People talk all the time about being real. John embodies realness. With John, you're going to know what's on his mind because he will tell you. Not in a rude way. Quite the opposite, John is someone who you love having conversations with. There were times, in the office; an informal meeting or two when I might cringe knowing John was about to pipe in with something brash. In hindsight, it was some of those things he said that helped us build the foundation for the run we had covering the greatest sports city in America for nearly 2 decades. John, our fellow ENG Photographers (commonly known as "Videographers") and I didn't just go to these iconic sports events with our cameras and hit the record button. We prepared, we strategized, we studied, we paid attention, we kept the faith, and knew that anything could happen and we had to be ready. We thrived for and in the big games and the moments within those. We lived for and in each special moment. The big games you anticipated, the World Series, the Stanley Cup Playoffs, the Super Bowls, the NBA Finals, were OUR big games. We played off of each other and celebrated each other's victories, big and small and enjoyed every moment in between. We lamented on each other's failures, big and small. Most failures were small compared to the successes we enjoyed, but they were important nonetheless. We hated failing. But we learned from our mistakes (usually) and managed to have fun along the way. No doubt you'll read some of those stories in this book. We never stopped trying to get better and that drove us.

For John and I, it all started in the fall of 1996 when I became an intern at Cablevision of Boston / Brookline. I grew up in Boston and Brookline and had many of my high school games covered by Cablevision. My little league baseball coach was on the production crew there and helped me get an internship I needed to qualify for graduation. John started working there as part of our production crew soon after me in the spring of '97. We clicked right away. At that time, I was still a quiet, relatively reserved young man. I had achieved a few things, but didn't know how to use my successes to embolden my personality yet. John was the opposite. He was not shy. He was funny, brash and he was bold. At that time, he was still a bike courier in Boston, weaving through the remnants of Boston's "Big Dig" on a 10-speed, so he had to be aggressive. We covered all the high school sports events and politics for Boston and Brookline. We learned all parts of production and took direction from the Senior Producer, Chris Larson. Chris taught us a lot. He was very helpful and usually put us in the best positions to succeed. He quickly assessed that John and I excelled at the handheld camera position for games and concerts. That became a regular occurrence. Someone even coined us "The Handheld Brothers." "Someone" was probably the two of us. But we knew we were good and had something special going.

One of the great parts of working on those productions was the downtime after we had set up the equipment. That's when the basketballs and footballs came out to see who could make a half-court shot (me) or kick it through the goal post (sometimes John). We were all out there. For the most part, having not warmed up, we all failed miserably. But we laughed, man, did we laugh.

Chris rarely came out of the truck when prepping for a game. He was a great guy but he took his role as Director very seriously. I thank God for that because we all learned so much about professionalism from him. Without fail, however, as we were wrapping up our fun, John was always the last one attempting the FGs or one last shot. At least, it seemed that way to Chris, who would come out of the truck, red-faced, and holler in a grouchy growl, "JOHN GET OFF THE FIELD!!!" Every time, Chris would come out right when John had the ball in his hands or took that shot that ended up hitting a piece of equipment. We would laugh and say, "Yeah, John get off the field." He was snake bitten on the recreational aspect, but he was serious about his craft.

2007

Throughout the years I worked with him at Cablevision and then at NESN, John excelled as a shooter. Organized & hardworking, creative and meticulous with lighting and framing shots. Even though he was a steady shot on the shoulder, "Mr. Soft Hands" grizzled at the thought of a shooter leaving the shop without a tripod. "Don't be lazy," he would often say to me in the early years. Although, truth be told, I still prefer shooting off the shoulder (that's the stubborn artist/competitor in me), he was usually right. I probably could've saved a day of back pain or two had I listened. If you have time for the tripod, it is always best.

I'm realizing, I could write a whole book about John. I wouldn't be half the man I am today, were it not for John and our friendship. Whether we were working, playing softball, golfing, having some cold ones in a parking lot or when I really needed someone to tell me life was going to be okay, I always knew I could confide in him and he would have my back. And he did. But this is not my book! What I can tell you about this book is that it will be genuine and it will be fun. John loves great storytelling and is a great storyteller. That's probably why he has more friends over the age of 75 than anyone alive. Over the years, many of John's friends would become my friends. He brings people together that otherwise would never have anything in common. He's someone you want to be around and you gravitate towards. He's earned the nickname "The Mayor" many times for his ability to converse with anyone. "The Mayor of Fort Myers" (the Red Sox Spring Training home), is my favorite. His authenticity will have you burning through the pages ahead, as you get a unique, behind-the-scenes, look into the most iconic sports era of all time.

~ Patrick J. Gamere

CHAPTER 1

Cleveland Rocks

IT WAS A dark and not so stormy night in Cleveland, Ohio.

The pitcher in the game had thrown four wild pitches or pass balls. Depends who you ask. Perhaps it was a new catcher.

Shortly after the game, I was sitting in the hotel bar with some of our crew when the pitcher showed up. A short while later, after a few beverages, we were in a cab en route to a 'dance club' across town. Upon entering the club, the pitcher gave everyone in our party a $100 bill. Inside, all had a good time and upon leaving I handed him $47 in change. I believe I was the only one that returned some of the money. $53 buys a couple of beers and a nice dance! Certainly, a memorable night.

I told the pitcher the next day, both of us pretty hung over, last night's events would lead my book someday!

Pregame at Progressive Field

There was always something memorable about the city of Cleveland. It all stems from the first time I went there and saw a reporter from a Boston newspaper fall drunk off his barstool while covering an NCAA basketball tournament. I knew there was something about this town. I'm not saying Cleveland is a bad town. I actually have always enjoyed going there. There were many trips working baseball, football and basketball games. Even got to meet Allen Iverson one night after an NBA game. Well, my reporter, Jayme Parker, really wanted to meet him. So, we did.

It was also the city late in my career that my wife thought I only and exclusively traveled to. According to her, there was nowhere else in the US I covered games except Cleveland and sometimes Detroit!

Really not that bad a city for being so close to the 'ocean'! A lot of times we would stay at the Ritz and there was a great underground shopping mall right near the hotel. It was a great place to walk around in the mornings prior to heading over to the ballpark.

Also, one of my favorite sandwich shops was there. I think it was called Jake's. It was on the way to the ballpark and they made the best pastrami sandwich!

One also cannot forget Cleveland is home to the Rock and Roll Hall of Fame, which I tried to visit every time I was in town. One time, Joe Haggerty stood me up at the Hall. I really thought he was big leaguing me and just not showing up. We were going to go see a marvelous Grateful Dead exhibit that was on display there.

After I waited well over an hour, he finally got in touch with me and explained that he had been on the phone getting chewed out by the GM of the Red Sox. You see, Joe had written a small article the night before questioning some of the behavior of certain members of the team, I believe with references to frat boys or guys who attended weddings. Not sure, but I respected Joe because later that day he turned up in the Red Sox locker room to defend his article. Until that time I'd only seen one other writer, Steve Buckley (crushed Nomar) show up in the locker room to defend what he wrote. It takes guts to tell the truth and even more guts to show up and defend your work. Take note young journalists and bloggers. Too bad Joe missed a great exhibit but sometimes duty calls.

Progressive Field

In September of 2015, I was working our baseball's play-by-play man's Don Orsillo's last game at NESN. It was an emotional weekend and quite sad for everyone that our good friend was leaving us after many years of loyal service. He was his usual professional self and we had some good laughs with the Cleveland manager. Captured a very memorable moment of those two wrestling on tape! Hands and fingers going everywhere and probably where they shouldn't!

The good times really happened when I was packing my gear to head back on the charter flight to Boston. I would always work baseball games in civilian clothes and then change into a suit for the flight back home. No place to dress and our managers' office happened to be open; I suddenly had the perfect changing room. For a moment I felt like a big leaguer! Got to change somewhere! It should be noted that on that trip, someone paid for a small plane with a banner trailing off the back wishing DO the best! Very classy.

Speaking of former managers, years earlier when he was managing another ballclub I had a very weird experience in a hotel hallway with him. For some reason, he and I got off on the same floor and our rooms, remarkably, were right next to each other. It happened to be his birthday and there were three extremely good-looking people waiting in his room for him. What a birthday present! The funniest part was, they welcomed him by the wrong name, which he corrected them as the door was closing right in front of me. Realizing my room was right next to his I thought it was going to be a long and loud night when the phone suddenly rang and the front desk informed me I was in the wrong room. No kidding!

'High' 3rd

Sticking with baseball, I was working a very cold night at the ballpark and the cameraman next to me for the home broadcast show offered me to smoke a 'little something special'. To 'stay warm' I said yes. I swear he tried to drug me and I spent the rest of the night freezing, shivering and fearful that he was going to take advantage of me or something.

My director kept asking if I was OK and I wasn't. I got my head together by the end of the game, thank goodness for the usual three-and-a-half hour games, and was OK for my postgame duties. I saw that guy the next night and politely declined his offer. Never trust a stranger. Especially a cameraman in a gasoline station attendant's uniform in an empty third deck.

It was also at the ballpark, then Jacobs Field; former Red Sox PR man John Blake in '07 created the new Olympic event of couch throwing! It never really caught on after that trip.

I will always remember Cleveland because it was the last trip I took with the Red Sox before I went into retirement in the fall of 2016. The Red Sox were in the playoffs and I had a great time with our crew especially being with BryGuy, Dan Aspan and 'Papi' Narracci. We did our usual ass-kicking TV wise but for me, it was good just being there with them with the knowledge it was probably my last roadie and couldn't have been with better company.

Maybe someday the Celtics will figure out how to beat LeBron.

Cleveland rocks!

CHAPTER 2

In the Beginning

I HAD BEEN working as a bicycle messenger with my friend Owen Carlson for over 10 years when it dawned on me that I was fast approaching age 30 and it was time for a career change. Friends Rob Kirwan and Doug Rose were both working in different capacities in TV production at the time. Rob, an editor extraordinaire and Doug, a sports television cameraman were my inspiration and launching pad. I will forever be indebted to those two.

Early one morning I woke up and on WBCN FM 104—remember them? There was an ad during the *Howard Stern Show* for the Connecticut School of Broadcasting. I figured, what the heck, I'll give them a call. I was lucky enough to be accepted and attend this prestigious four-month trade school with the support and assistance from my friend Coco. Thank you!

Everyone who attended there had aspirations of being a sports television broadcaster. Not judging. I was the only person there with behind the camera production interests. There was only one class, taught by John Upton, on television production. I will never forget it. In that class, the best advice he gave was to find a job at a local cable company. To this day, John is still the man showing up at venues with the cutest of interns sharing his knowledge.

Luckily, I had been playing softball with a guy named Victor Brown who was a cable repo man. No bullshit. He got me in touch with Chris Larson of Cablevision in Brookline / Boston and there my TV career began.

I will never forget sitting in front of Chris Larson and asking him for an internship which he could not give me because CSB was not an accredited school. He then looked at me and said 'but we can hire you for $10 an hour!' Okay, I'm in!

What an outstanding first job in television. We did everything from high school sports (some really bad) to political events to a live children's call-in homework help show. You name it we did it. Most shows were 'live to tape' and we worked in a forum where you could make mistakes and learn and grow professionally, although mistakes were not encouraged.

The first event I ever shot for Cablevision was a Brookline High boys and girls hockey doubleheader at Boston Univesity's Walter Brown Arena. Funny it was there because twenty years earlier I had gone to a Boston Lobsters tennis event with my mom. We saw Bud Collins, who wrote for the Boston Globe, and I thought then how cool sports in big arenas really were.

Of course, during game number two, the wide shot camera which I built earlier collapsed halfway through the first period as I did not gaff tape the tripod well enough. Condensation at work. I never admitted my first TV blunder to Chris.

The beauty of working in TV production is when you make a mistake you rarely make it a second time or you're really bad or a complete idiot. We've all worked with both!

Chris Larson was a great early mentor. For some reason, I always seemed to get in trouble with him but I believe we both had a mutual respect for one another. I know I always respected him.

Chris was a huge Who and Bruins fan and passed away during the 2011 Bruins Stanley Cup campaign. I often thought of him and felt what a terrible time to check out as he loved the B's. He was in my thoughts during their playoff run and every game I ever worked as an event camera operator as I could always hear him in my headset telling me to pay attention and focus!

I worked with so many great people there and have so many great memories of all the outstanding shoots and productions we worked on. There is such great camaraderie in television at least between the production crew. The relationship between the front office and the production crew is a little different. Apples and oranges. Many thanks to all the Cablevision crew, Arlen Showstack, Joy Shaughnessy, Camy Locks and Joanne Brown to name a few. Those were some great times!

A slight programming interruption.

It should be known that ten years earlier in 1987 before I ever considered working in television an old college roommate, Scott, and I attended two tapings of the then-popular WBZ TV show called *People Are Talking*. It was free to sit in the studio audience so we did! This is not one of those I was 'destined to work in TV' moments but it's actually quite hilarious.

The first show we attended was about an apparel line for larger ladies. The host, Tom Bergeron, would walk in the audience soliciting questions. I will never forget making a statement to Tom of 'how well all the ladies looked.' Tom looked quizzically at me with a look of are you kidding me!

The funny part of that show was my brother Jim was at home watching it live and every time they cut to Tom there was Scott and I giggling behind him!

People Are Talking 1987

The second show we attended the guest was Vanna White. She was promoting a book, and I guess she had just been in Playboy with some photos that she was not too proud of. Attending these tapings was the first time I was ever in a TV studio and I remember it being pretty cool. The Vanna show is on YouTube somewhere!

Back to the story . . .

After three years of shooting everything under the sun, literally, with Cablevision I was fortunate enough to get a job at NESN—the New England Sports Network: home of the Boston Red Sox and Boston Bruins—as a Master Control operator with the promise that I would soon move into a position in their videography department.

Nancy Rose hired me in November 1998 and to this day I may still be the worst master control operator that ever worked there, or in television history. I was hired at $6.50 an hour and couldn't have been happier. One month later Nancy walked into the master control room and gave me a $50 Christmas bonus. Back then, that was a lot of money! Thank you, Nancy, for taking a chance on me.

Within a year of working there, NESN's two main photographers left for better gigs. The door was wide open for me and my friend, Patrick Gamere, to become NESN's full-time cameramen. Pat and I had been together since Cablevision and had formed a great friendship and professional relationship. It made sense to bring him in and for us to continue what would turn out to be nineteen years of working together and a boatload of memories!

Man, we had some great times. You have to be good friends with someone if you ask them to write the forward of your book!

JPM & Patrick Gamere

Pat and I have been joined at the hip since we first met at Cablevision. There, we became the famed 'handheld brothers' and it seems our lives have paralleled themselves since. We even got married within a week of each other in 2001. We have been there for each other through our entire professional development, the ups and downs, the championships and everything in between. We were fortunate to always have each other not only professionally but personally over the years!

I'll express many times in this book that working the big games with him, Bryan Brennan, Chris DelDotto, and Eric Scharmer were the best of times.

The beauty of my time at NESN with Pat was he and I single-handedly built the photography department with the help and guidance of Eric Scharmer, who was another great mentor for me. That shop was our creation and we had complete control of it although middle management did attempt to 'peek' in the window time and again.

The Photography Shop—NESN

My first ever shot for NESN could not have gone any worse. My first real chance to show them what I've got, what I was made of. It was a *Front Row* story on a woman named Nicole Barber, coach of a high school boys hockey team somewhere in RI.

Here we are, in my wife Adrienne's car, Producer Sarge, aka Todd

Kerrissey, PA Michael Fericano and myself speeding towards the shoot when I drive by an A/V store on Rte 95, and realize I've forgotten to pack tape for the camera. Tape, meaning recording tape, meaning Beta recording tape. Uh oh.

I quickly pulled off the highway, explained to my coworkers what was happening and headed towards said A/V store. There, no luck, only Beta machines for sale. Uh oh.

Now running late, we decide we'll drive to the shoot and on our way concoct a full proof story. We're basically going to show up and lie. Upon arrival, Sarge and Mike go in and stall for time while I was at the car.

Seven and a half short minutes later I walk in, disheveled, and inform everyone 'the drive train motor mechanism is inoperative!' Sounded good to me and they believed it! We rescheduled for two weeks later and I managed to bring Beta tape with us. In fact, I never once forgot tape again throughout my entire career.

The shoot happened and proved to me I was nowhere near qualified to be a cameraman at this level. The interviews looked terrible. Nicole's interview was shot shooting up to her face with a milky white sky as an infinite backdrop. The headmasters interview was him placed in front of a huge stained-glass school insignia. Totally backlit. Both interviews had lens back focus issues which made them instantly soft (or out of focus). Luckily, the B-roll I shot was somewhat usable.

I learned more on those shoots, one really, that really humbled me and motivated me more than ever to get back out there and give it another shot. No pun intended. The *Front Row* producers were very patient.

I knew I was a terrible Master Control op—I had to become a better shooter. Slowly, Nancy scheduled me to more and more shoots and I started to get more comfortable with the gear and my confidence started to grow.

Then Mike Cole gave me the sequencing lesson. We were at the studios one day and he asked me if I knew how to shoot a sequence. Of course not, I answered and he motioned me to sit down at one of the upright tape machines. He told me to sit there and rewind a tape back and forth which I dutifully did.

As I toggled the rewind wheel back and forth, Mike shot me as he did a half circle behind me and to the side of the deck. When he finished we watched the tape he shot. What was on it instantly changed the way I approached shooting.

Mike taped me performing one action. On the tape were ten different shots of me performing that one action. One angel wide, the establishing shot. A couple mediums of the tape deck and my face. Then a bunch of tight shots, some really tight. Hands on the dial, eyes, numbers on the deck.

And kapow, I got it. Wide, medium and tight. That's a sequence. Pretty simple stuff. Who knew?

Mike was an early mentor to me who helped me grow immeasurably. He was born to shoot *Front Row*. He owned that show. He remains a gifted photographer to this day and is still an avid Rush fan.

Early in my career, I was balancing jobs between still being a bicycle messenger one day a week with working for Cablevision and NESN. I was very busy and super focused.

My wife Adrienne was incredibly supportive during this time, as I would make her watch Brookline girls' field hockey on TV when it was posted for broadcast. There are not a whole lot of people that would actually do that with you. She did.

I could go on and on but that's basically the foundation of the beginning.

CHAPTER 3

Talent: The Most Misused Word in the Business

OKAY, THE GLOVES are off!

This chapter is dedicated respectfully to many of the on-air people I have had the benefit of working with. There are a couple ways to go about this: I could write everybody's name and then critique them and go on and on, but instead, I will just simply call out a few of the more memorable individuals I had the pleasure of working with.

If you're an on-air personality and do not see your name mentioned here it's either because I don't like you or I simply didn't get to you but please take no offense. I can honestly say that I enjoyed working with all the people I came across during my career, with the possible exception of one. You know who you are. No need to beat a dead horse or should I say a former washed up beauty queen.

Charlie, hang tight, you're getting a whole chapter!

I'll begin with my second shoot at NESN. It was with Bruins legend & TV 38 star Tom Larson. We were heading out for a *Front Row* (more on that show later) shoot in Southbridge, Massachusetts to cover a story on a dog behaviorist.

Here I am in Adrienne's car with Tom thinking how cool this is going be, being on my first shoot with this legend of local television. As I tell him that I also work at Cablevision, he angrily tells me how he paid his cable bill with a bag of change and made that bitch behind the counter count every cent of it! That was ten miles into our trip and I was figuring I had possibly made the wrong decision to go on this shoot.

The shoot turned out fine and I continued to have a great run of over ten years with Tom. We covered all kinds of stories and events for *Front Row* and every shoot and experience with him was memorable.

Not long after his unceremonious departure from the Network, I produced a short film about him and his relationship with the many camera ops he worked with. It was called *The Larson Project* and if you really want to see it or consider yourself a fan of Tom's, give me a call. I'm biased but I think it's pretty entertaining.

What made time great with Tom was his ability for great storytelling coupled with his honesty and delivery. "In the end. . . . . . ." should be his signature line! We remain friends today and our friendship means a lot to me.

Like with most sports networks, I worked with a gaggle of sideline reporters beginning with TC—Tom Caron, Eric Frede and what seemed to be an endless parade of talented women that came through the door. TC was the original sideline guy and he'll tell you he remains the best. Debatable? Perhaps. Honestly, TC is as solid as they come. He really can do it all and is a great friend. He can give you 'man on the street' or play by play or a quick VO if need be. He'll outwork anyone. But if he's one thing—he is genuine and professional. Okay, that's two.

Later in my career I really enjoyed working the MLB Winter Meetings with Tom. It was the one time of year where we could work for five days together, get sick of each other, have a great time, get sick of each other again and then reconnect a year later. Always memorable times and I hope his knee heels up someday.

Talent at work

After TC was done with the sideline gig, Eric Frede stepped in and it was truly a pleasure to work with Eric for the two or three years he was at the Network. He too can do it all and is a true professional and an outstanding human being.

Now for the sideline gals! There will always be two that really stick out in my mind as great friends and true professionals. Tina Cervasio with baseball and Naoko Funayama with hockey. These two set the bar in regards to friendship and professionalism.

First, one must understand that the photographer/reporter relationship in any aspect of TV sports or news production can be a very close one. It can be a great working relationship or a disaster. Believe me, I've experienced both.

Working with these two was like working with my two best friends! We worked hard. We worked long hours. And I was never prouder to have worked with both of them.

It was my pleasure to watch them develop and grow professionally. Not to mention we had some great times together! I had the pleasure of working with Tina when the Red Sox won it all in '07 and with Naoko when the Bruins won it all in '11. Certainly, memorable times not to mention all the practices, car rides and coffees in between. Tina is currently ruling the NYC airwaves and NFR is a proud mom of two and still in the TV biz.

Tina offers instruction

Of all the Naoko stories I could tell and there are hundreds, I've always loved this one.

We're in Sunrise, FL working a Panthers game and it's a dual feed broadcast. That means both the home and away TV productions share the same truck and some cameras. Sometimes I was the odd man out and not scheduled to work the game itself. No biggie, kind of nice to get time in between pre and postgame and enjoy the game.

So, I'm sitting with NFR rink side watching the game and spot the Jumbotron camera guy right near us. I lean over and ask him if he's one of the guys that shoot fans during the 'Kiss Cam' segment of the night. You've seen it. We've all seen it and you can't keep your eyes from it because you love it. Yes, you do.

The cameraman acknowledges yes and I motion to NFR who is unaware of our brief conversation. A few moments later I ask Naoko if she's ever been on the Kiss Cam and given the opportunity, if by some act of God, she and I were to be on such a thing what would our plan be.

Through all this, she remains absolutely clueless to this setup. Together we decide a handshake wouldn't work, neither would a peck on the cheek. We agree that a European kiss on each cheek would be the most proper. She still has no idea what's coming. By now, I know you know, so . . .

It comes to that magical point in the game. I'm ready, my camera guy's ready, cut to US! I tap NFR and point to the Jumbotron and she has no choice but to go through with it. Our European peck on each cheek was flawless and we enjoyed a good laugh afterward. Some people wait a lifetime for that kind of moment, I kind of manufactured it.

Fast forward to postgame and upon entering the Bruins locker room Johnny Boychuck yells out, "Naoko! kissy kissy kissy!" The whole room breaks up because everyone watches the Kiss Cam. Players, fans and even coaches because when we got on the team bus later, Doug Jarvis (NHL Ironman & Bruins coach) looks at NFR and says, "Hey, I saw you on TV tonight in the rink, looking good."

NFR interviews Patrice Bergeron

Later sideline talent included Jenny Dell and Jamie Erhdahl. I loved working with those two. Equally as professional and talented as Tina and Naoko, and both are enjoying national network careers. Many a great time with both! No doubt!

Can't forget to mention Heidi Watney here as well. She had the longest tenure of any sideline reporter of five years and no championships. Sorry HW. We did have some good times.

Sarah Davis, Elle Duncan, and Gary Striewski were talented individuals and great friends! Sarah worked as the B's sideline reporter and did a fabulous job. I had a terrific time working and hanging out with her. We'll always have Nashville SD! Elle and Gary are talented beyond belief and have both moved on to national gigs.

Bob Rogers. Now there's an interesting character. Hosted a sports highlight show at the Network for a number of years and in the spring of 2004 was dispatched to Fort Myers to cover Red Sox spring training. At some point during spring training, it was more important for him to go home to Massachusetts and coach his high school basketball team, which he was told not to do. Well, he did it anyway and his team lost and he eventually lost his job paving the way for the gargantuan success that TC has turned into today.

Bob was told by management not to leave and we tried to stop him too but he did, and it cost him working the now fabled 2004 World Series run!

Darn near almost cost me my job as well. I hear he is still coaching and I hope that's going well for him. He was a solid TV man who believed more in his team than his employer ultimately believed in him.

Sports Desk, or whatever that show was ever called at any point, produced a bunch of anchors and reporters. As I said, I will not mention them all here. But a few come to mind.

Randy Scott, John Chandler and Paul Devlin, all great guys and solid reporters. Paul and I worked the Patriots '06 season together. We did some great stuff. You may remember Paul as Charlie Higgins from the 1988 movie *Bull Durham*. He was the lefty that took Tim Robbins deep! I think to this day he is still collecting a royalty check. Lots of travel with Paul. The most memorable memory I have with Paul was our fascination with the machine that moved the Jersey barriers along Route 93. We would marvel every time we were driving back from practice and saw this magnificent invention perform its magic.

John, a native Clevelander, was a great friend and is a gifted TV person. I always enjoyed working with him and we did some great stuff over the years including the Celtics championship in 2008. And Randy, who I met in Fort Myers way back when he was at WINK is now a big shot at ESPN. You will not meet a nicer guy in the business and he has a fine shoe collection of which I'm sure he is quite proud.

In 2004, on our Red Sox pregame show, I worked with Boston local comedian Jimmy Dunn. Jimmy hosted a show called Fan Attic and also did bits on our pregame show. He was hilarious.

I will never forget doing a corked bat segment at the top of the Red Sox dugout when Terry Francona came out and saw us with a one-inch drill bit and a bunch of balls trying to stuff them in a hollowed out baseball bat. All the balls fell out and rolled right to his feet and we all cracked up!

Funny Ball, a book, was Jim's attempt to cash in, like everybody else, on the Sox success in '04 and can probably be purchased online somewhere or found at your local library!

Jimmy still regularly performs at the Kowloon in Saugus, MA and is available for private parties or functions. I get no cut for that shameless promotion, by the way.

Now to the broadcast teams. Jack and Brick. Don and Jerry. For a long time, I've been on the record stating that Phil Leggitt and Paul Sherwin are the best play-by-play duo in sports television and I stand by that assertion. No offense gentlemen. They host the Tour de France every year, and in my opinion, that is the greatest month of the television.

Here locally we have Jack Edwards and Andy Brickley handling the hockey broadcast and had Don Orsillo and Jerry Remy (Dave O'Brien is now in there) with the baseball. All great guys, super knowledgeable and a true pleasure to work with. Jack may be the smartest human being I've ever met. Brick is not far behind him so far as life lessons and hockey knowledge. And a big fan of Johnny Cash! And who else do you know that has actually met Bob Dylan!

Don Orsillo. Many a great time was spent with Don over the years. At the ballpark, on the charters, on the road, at the pool bronzing and of course, hanging in the booth. DO is a top-notch play-by-play man and good friend!

Two vivid memories working with Don stand out. Funny enough those are around the first time I met Don and the last time I worked with him. First, we invited him on the Charlie Moore Outdoor Show. We were basically introducing Don to Red Sox nation. Little did people know he was an avid fisherman. We had a great day on the boat that day and an even better time at dinner afterward. Angela and Charlie cooked up a fine lobster meal.

The second memory was when Don hosted us for dinner during spring training of 2015. You must understand, Don was never seen away from the ballpark during spring training. Ever.

He rented a condo in a secret location outside of Fort Myers that no one knew about. The invite came out of nowhere as a group of us were invited for drinks and dinner with DO and his girlfriend Kathy. What a great night! Fine drinks, an amazing surf and turf meal, and cigars with dessert!

If you follow Don on any social media platform you may also know him as Donatangelo, a world-class chef, and wine enthusiast. They certainly did not disappoint that night, as it was a great evening for the crew to get together, enjoy each other's company and have some laughs.

I worked the 2015 season with Don and then he was off to San Diego. It was truly my pleasure working with all four of those guys. I learned so much and was always appreciative to work with such greatness!

Rob Simpson. Simmer. The brains behind The Biscuit. He was the Bruins rinkside reporter for three seasons and the producer/host of Rubber Biscuit. Rubber Biscuit was a magazine type show and really a throwback to the old *Front Row* days. Sarge producing, Kevin Newton editing and the Photogs shooting, doing our thing. Meanwhile, every episode of The Biscuit was upstairs in Rob's head just floating around.

We would shoot elements in four different cities and would never have a script or shot sheet. Rob is a great storyteller and he was always two or three moves ahead of himself.

The show consisted of hockey features on players, cities of interest and the outright abstract. It was right up our alley and we all enjoyed working on that show!

I really enjoyed working with Rob because he was one of the few remaining risk takers in television and in life for that matter. He wasn't afraid to try something and have it turn out to be a complete piece of shit. It didn't matter. I always respected him for that. These days, Rob is up in Toronto working in radio, writing books and still having fun.

One thing NESN has always done well was to have former players work in an analyst position for the pre and postgame shows. Dennis Eckersley, Jim Rice, Steve Lyons for baseball, and Barry Pederson and Rick Middleton for hockey to name a few are great guys and it was awesome to not only meet them but to work with them. Shooting a documentary on Jim Rice in his hometown of Anderson, South Carolina with Gara and then playing golf with Jim will forever be a cherished memory. We were the first TV crew to ever tell his story from his hometown. It was a great honor. And Eck! What can you say? He is so fucking cool!

And of course, I can't forget KTap—Katherine Tappen. Such a great person. Such a great talent. Such a great friend. I truly enjoyed working with her and could not be prouder of the success she has become at NBC. Every time I see her on TV I just beam with pride. The Network should have never let her get away. Good for her!

So, if I worked with you and didn't mention your name I apologize. Some would contend you could write an entire book on Mike Perlow or you could buy his book. Just can't get to everybody.

CHAPTER 4

The Network

THIS CHAPTER WILL offer a brief description of the Network (NESN) and some general thoughts, observations and musings.

NESN was created in 1984 to carry the Boston Red Sox and the Boston Bruins games on cable TV. The station is owned eighty percent by the Boston Red Sox and the other twenty percent by the Boston Bruins if that math still stands. Who knows?

If you're really interested in the history of the station watch *NESN 30* which I shot with producer Steve Garabedian. It pretty much tells the story of the station.

The show should have been sponsored by The Ninety-Nine Restaurant. I can't remember how many meals we ate there during production. It was a lot considering some interviews we needlessly had to reshoot. The Ninety-Nine—You'll always come back for more!

The Network covers the six-state New England region and even has a national channel. I don't think they carry the pro-product games though. Its history is really quite impressive starting as a small pay-by-season for Red Sox or Bruins games or both to a huge chip in the sale of the Boston Red Sox in 2003.

When I arrived in the fall of 1998, there were probably no more than fifty people working there. Today there's close to two hundred. The station really took off after the 2004 Red Sox World Series victory and becoming available on your basic cable package.

The greatest asset of NESN is the fine people that work there. I was always appreciative of the outstanding production people that I had a chance to work with and make some great television. As I said earlier there is great camaraderie in TV.

The Network was always good to me. Every year I made more money than the year before, enjoyed great benefits and every year added more experiences to my trunk load of memories. Or as I would often say, 'every shoot I just keep adding to my legacy!'

Coordinating producer Steve Sera had conviction and guts. Steve is one of a kind or should I say 'a stampede of one.' He was one of the first coordinating producers I worked for at NESN.

What I most respected about working for Steve was he was honest. Straight to the chase—truly honest. He would stand up to anybody for his people and that goes a long way. I would love going to his desk and reporting that I was down to my last thirty-minute beta tape and he would run down the hall and implore people demanding that we purchase more tape!

Steve has always been in the A/V world. If you don't believe me just visit Axminster on YouTube—*Hands Wettin' the Wheel* may be the best one. Giddy up!

Steve was the coordinating producer on *Front Row* and then on the pre and postgame show as well as numerous other productions. I will always appreciate the day Steve took me, Pat Gamere and Nancy Rose across the street to the Boston Beer Works and really gave it to us good, Pat and me that is. We were shooting the Fast Track race car show and not doing so good a job. We were not shooting up to the standard that was expected. The standard photographers Mike Cole and Sal Malguarnera set. Steve really handed it to us and challenged us to be better than what we were delivering. It hurt at the moment to hear that you're not good. Nobody ever wants to hear that. He knew we were better and I will never forget his honesty. It made better photographers of both Patrick and myself.

Everybody I knew there brought their best skill sets to the table. I always felt NESN was a good fit for local people who did not want to deal with the machine of ESPN down in Bristol, Connecticut. Especially in the early days, during the *Front Row* period, it really was the golden age of television for a bunch of us.

Inside the Network

Front Row, you ask? A four-letter word to some, but to a handful of us it was and remains one of the greatest productions we ever worked on. Originally formed as a half an hour magazine show prior to the Red Sox telecast, *Front Row* became a great venue for storytelling. It was like WCVB's *Chronicle* but rather about sports. We would produce stories from two and a half minutes to a full half hour. We were storytellers. And we would tell anyone's story anywhere throughout New England. The beauty of that show was no one was telling us how to shoot it, how to write or edit it. There were some amazing individuals that worked on that program. Steve Sera, Peter Frechette, Mike Cole, Sal Malguarnera, Eric Scharmer, Sarge, Kevin Newton, Bob Sylvester, Patrick Gamere and Jim Carroll to just name a few. There were many others!

Front Row was more than just a show to many of us. It allowed us to fully tap into our creative identity and we had full reign and freedom to do whatever we wanted to. It won a ton of awards and to this day holds a special place in all our hearts. Unfortunately, the Network did not feel the same way we did and the show at one point was retooled to an hour-long documentary show.

That's when I was hitting my stride at NESN as a videographer and the first show I shot entirely on my own was a Johnny Ruiz documentary. Johnny was a local boxer from Chelsea who was training to fight Evander Holyfield for the third time in Las Vegas. We spent six months training with him (shooting that is) and then went to Vegas. What a week.

Producer Bob Sylvester and I along with Tom Larson were out in Vegas for a week, and he won the fight, which made our show even that much better. Unfortunately, the show lost out at the NE/Boston Emmy awards to Charlie Moore fishing with Ted Nugent. Oh well, I guess you can't compete with Uncle Ted.

Bob Sylvester and I also had a long history together at the Network. I worked with Bob during my early days on *Front Row* and then for ten years on the Charlie Moore show, which I'll get into later. Bob is another top producer and good friend, and he and I enjoyed many years making great TV together. He was also hired at first as a Master Control operator but I'm pretty confident he was nowhere near as incompetent as I was. Like a lot of people in my early days there, he was very patient and was extremely helpful bringing me along as a young photographer. I may have burned him pretty good on the Kendo feature but I always worked hard for him.

The new format of *Front Row* produced sixteen one-hour shows. The first one we rolled out was a behind the scenes documentary with the Boston Bruins called *To Bleed Black and Gold*. Much like the 24/7 shows that are produced today that show was a trailblazer. It's interesting; there is a lot of television on today that we did back then. Who knew we were our own television trailblazers?

Another notable show was titled *Diamonds in the Far East-Baseball in Japan*. Producer Bob Sylvester, Jim Van Dillon, an interpreter and I spent ten days in Japan in late May 2002. We hit the ground running and shot in six cities over a ten-day period. We worked with Tuffy Rhoades and legend Sadaharu Oh.

On our last night in Japan Bob, Jim and I treated ourselves to a lovely night out. After dinner at a fine Japanese restaurant and a few stops in between, we walked out of the last bar at sunrise feeling like we had done Tokyo justice. An entire movie could be made about three Americans riding in an elevator with a 5' 5" Japanese fella! The trip was an experience of a lifetime and we were all pleased and very proud to win an Emmy award for that one!

I could go on and on and on about the *Front Row* days but do not want to bore you too much. To this day, working on that show remains by far my proudest accomplishment at the Network.

After *Front Row* was gassed due to the lack of effort in trying to sell it, things started to change. As with a lot of sports television in today's world, it became more about B-roll and talking heads. That's easy television to produce and less expensive. It takes too much time and effort to tell a good story these days. How unfortunate. *Front Row* could have easily been sold and would have had an enormous audience if properly marketed. I know it did when we made it.

I mentioned Nancy Rose earlier. She not only hired me, but Bob Sylvester and many others over the years. She meant a great deal to NESN and to the many of us who served time there. She was NESN! An equal opportunity human being is she. A term of endearment I coined after Nancy left the station was 'The Nancy Boys.' This was for the group, all good guys for the most part, who took over NJR's primary functions after she departed the Network. In her prime, she really did it all. Scheduling, programming, running Master Control, and the list goes on. To me, it's a true testament to her ability and contributions that it took so many to replace her greatness.

So, the day-to-day assignments at NESN became more of hanging around locker rooms waiting for overpaid and whiny athletes to talk about how good they were or how bad the other guy was.

Waiting for greatness. *Blah blah blah*. You could actually see the creative juices literally escaping from everybody. Good thing we still had the Charlie Moore show. (Yes, Charlie, stay with me; I'll get to you shortly!) The photographers started to travel more and do more event camera coverage. I'll delve into the travel aspect in the next chapter.

The Photography Department at this point consisted of me, Pat Gamere, Chris DelDotto, and Bryan Brennan.

A quick thought on the BryGuy. Certainly, one of the funniest people I know. Not sure when we hired him, not even sure when he left but what I can say is the entire time he was there things were never boring. Bryan brought great energy to our department and was a founding member of the Fun Bunch. He worked as hard as we all did, well most of the time but he was always about making sure that we were enjoying ourselves. After all, it's sports television. BryGuy is a true team player and road trips were always enjoyable with him.

Chris DelDotto, aka DelDots, I actually hired him around '04 and he's been a mainstay since. Great guy and a talented shooter!

We prided ourselves on having the same skill set as the next guy. That worked, most of the time. The four of us were a group that took care of each other, worked well together and were a true unit. We always had each other's back, considered ourselves an autonomous democracy and rarely a complaint was made of our group. It was ours. We knew it, they knew it and everybody knew it. A trip to our shop was a welcomed break from your day. To a man, I know we were all very proud to be part of that group.

The Photography Department

Over the course of my time at NESN, I made a few attempts at becoming the chief of the photography department. Management, in general, never cared for that word feeling that it sounded more like a Union term but I never agreed with that. I knew and everyone knew that I was the chief of that shop even if I never had the official title. I took it upon myself to constantly update, care, clean, maintain the gear and have control of the room. I was happy to do it. I know the guys were happy that I was happy to do it. After all, what's a fancy title and a few more thousand bucks every year?

It was pretty funny (strange not haha) that over my time there almost every annual review I ever had resulted in me being cited for violating the dress code policy. I liked to wear shorts during the warmer months and I was always cited for it in my review. It was hot, jeans simply weren't cutting it and I have/had good-looking legs (so the ladies say). Still got my three percent every year.

I also seemed to get in trouble quite often for apparently not having the best communication skills with middle management. I was told that I needed to be a more effective communicator with them where really it was me just expressing myself and offering my opinion on how things could be done differently in certain situations.

TV stations consist of two primary groups: front office/sales and production. There are the people who make it and the people that sell it, simple as that. Creative types versus number crunchers. It's ok to disagree. It's ok for conflict. Conflict can lead to resolution. The creative processes can have several right answers and several wrong ones. The journey to get there is sometimes necessary. I spent most of my time out in the field and a lot of those guys had not been outside of a twelve-foot x twelve-foot box in a great number of years. So, for me, offering different or constructive ways of doing things differently was perceived as me not respecting them or having poor communication skills. Untrue.

KSull, Blaney & BryGuy

While working at NESN, I met and had the privilege of working with a lot of great players on the Sox and Bruins. Ray Bourque was just at the end of his B's career before heading off to Colorado when I started. Over the course of nineteen years there were many, many players that came and went but two really stand out: Patrice Bergeron and Shawn Thornton.

Patrice started his Bruins career when he was eighteen years old, so I feel like I knew him the entire time he was with the Bruins. At least while I was with the Bruins. He is a great and talented hockey player but an even nicer human being. All in all, I've always found the hockey guys to be more relatable and friendlier than the baseball guys. I ended up working with Patrice on a few projects away from the rink including an Emmy winning commercial we shot and some elements for the *Bruins All Access* show. He was a lot younger then, so the Bruins made him available for that kind of stuff.

Another Bruin I became friendly with was Shawn Thornton. Anyone who works in the Boston sports media scene will tell you that Shawn was unlike any other athlete they have covered. And I agree.

Most athletes don't really talk too much to the local media except for some of the old-school reporters that they had established really tight relationships with. But Shawn would talk with anyone and everyone. Much like myself. Often times at the TD Garden, when we were in our third-floor studio Shawn would come in and hang out with us prior to game time. What athlete does that?

When the Bruins won the Stanley Cup in 2011 the first person that greeted me in the locker room was Patrice with a huge 'Johnny Martin!' That made me feel pretty good. Then I locked eyes with Shaun and he asked me where our reporter Naoko was. I then followed them as he doused her with a nice cold bottle of champagne in celebration!

Great guys. Most of the Bruins were great guys. Love the hockey guys. Claude Julien, the Bruins head coach for a number of years, was also a great guy and super to work with. When the Bruins had lost game six of the Stanley Cup Playoffs in 2013, Jack and Brick were interviewing Claude. At the conclusion of the interview, when everyone was wishing each other a pleasant off-season, Claude looked up at me through four people and said, "Scared you pretty good this morning didn't I?"

Earlier that day in the morning skate I'd gone down to the ice level to shoot Claude holding a meeting with the team and he immediately barked at me to leave the area to which I proceeded to run up the stairs. I should've been there in the first place. But how funny is that? This guy just lost in the Stanley Cup final and got eliminated, but remembers something that happened with the cameramen that morning!

Claude says hello

Notable Red Sox that I enjoyed being around was Tim Wakefield and Mike Timlin. I had the pleasure of working the Charlie Moore show with Tim and shot a hunting show with Tim and Mike after the '04 championship season.

Mike voiced the Alaska baseball film for us and did a fantastic job. More on that coming up. It's funny how after you work with someone away from the ballpark or hockey rink that you see them as real human beings instead of athletes. The thing is, pro athletes are continually bombarded with all kinds of requests. Interview requests, ticket requests, and appearances. It never ends.

I've noticed as players rise up the ranks of a professional franchise they slowly began to shut down emotionally and say no to all the requests, creating reputations for not being as accommodating, as maybe they should be. That's how some feel.

But working with these guys away from the ballpark or the hockey rink they were different people and I was glad I had those opportunities to be around them and get to know them on a different level.

Another great Red Sox player I enjoyed being around was David Ortiz. Who wouldn't? David has a very warm personality and he was very easy to talk to when you could get near him! That's of course if you could get near him. He always had a large crowd around him. But over the years we had some great chats and some good laughs. In his final season with the Red Sox in 2016, NESN, like everyone else, got in line to do their definitive final David Ortiz show. The network ended up getting two shows out of the interview that we did with David.

TC, David & JPM / the other 28 not pictured

Tom Caron did the interviews and did a fantastic job. The interview was shot at Fenway Park in late August and I believe I counted at least thirty NESN employees at the shoot. That's a lot of cooks! Back in the old days, there would've been two or three camera operators, a producer and the interviewer. This was a different time period where at times a lot of people, maybe too many, were thrown at a particular production. People were walking around with headsets like they worked at The Gap! Nonetheless, the interviews looked great and the shows, not sure which one, won a regional Emmy award although not all thirty participants who worked the shoot and beyond received an award. Only a select few. Hmmm.

Another great shoot I had with David was around the 2003 season which Tom Glennon produced. It was David and former Red Sox slugger, Sam Horn, cooking in the smallest of galley kitchens in an apartment building downtown.

Picture those two large guys with me and a camera trying to get shots of them and the food they were preparing. We shot Sam preparing three or four different dishes and watched him drink what appeared to be approximately twenty Coors Lights during the making of it. Stone cold sober the whole time.

The end of the shot was the most hilarious as David gave Sam a big bear hug, gave me a half a hug and then looked at Tom and patted him on the shoulder. Outta hugs, sorry Tommy! Those were the days when we were still shooting different and unique features for the pregame show.

One of the last Bruins shoots I ever did at NESN was a preseason gig where the team was invited to the NESN Television Center for media day. Media Day is the one time of the year where you can get the guys doing several different things for on-camera purposes. In one room a player would talk directly into the camera. In another room, the player would do moves with his stick, put his helmet on or adjust his gloves. Stuff like that.

Our room was a brief sit-down interview room. Bethany Marshall coordinated Media Day every year and always did a fantastic job. I always enjoyed doing the interview room as I took great pride in how good it looked with our Bruins backdrops. The interviews were no longer than five to ten minutes and usually focused around pop culture or things for the upcoming season. In the room with me was Amy Johnson; a young up-and-coming star at the Network conducting the interviews and in the corner of the room was Jack Edwards working on a project of proper name pronunciation. Leave it to Jack to trailblaze a project like that so announcers could always correctly pronounce players names. As I look back on it now, it was a great couple of days hanging out with Jack and having some good laughs. And of course, getting some quality work done.

Steve Garabedian. Gara, and I have been on more shoots than either us could probably count. I worked with Steve for over ten years and have pretty much done at all in regards to TV production with him. We've had some great times he and I! We've traveled all over the country together and have collaborated on several great projects.

Memorable ones include the Jim Rice show we shot in Anderson, South Carolina, the two NHL Hall of Fame induction shows (Bourque and Neely) and the Red Sox All Access features in Fort Myers. That doesn't even scratch the surface of the hundreds of interviews and features we've done and the countless miles we traveled.

Steve is a top-notch producer for a plethora of reasons. He may have the best working knowledge of past and present athletes and has a great vault of old-school video to back it up. There aren't many guys left like Steve in today's modern television world. Most of the young producers today have no knowledge of their local teams or athletes' past or present. It is glaringly obvious how much that can handicap them. Steve is the link between the past and the present. A true valuable asset. Outside of all this, Gara is a great friend and I enjoyed all the long car rides, all the shoots and most importantly our friendship over the years

Another friend and a quality broadcast engineer that keeps it all together at NESN to this day is Rob Serret, my favorite Dominican. Rob and I go back as far as Patrick Gamere and I do. Rob, Patrick and I were all at Cablevision together in the late 90's. During our time there, we worked on hundreds of in studio and remote shoots. Rob was there for all of them.

I brought Rob, like Pat, over to the Network along the way. Still waiting for my bonuses on those two and for my tenth and fifteenth-anniversary tchotchkes. Robbie is a quality human being and a loyal employee. He is also an avid old school Star Trek fan. How can you not love the guy!

Today the network still covers all the Red Sox and Bruins games quite well I would say and produces a couple of its own shows but nothing like the golden days. It has been suggested over time the station exists primarily for the two pro teams and could run color bars the rest of the time but that would put a lot of quality people out of work.

A quick nod to all my friends in the sales department. All great people! My good friend Tanya Mitchell single-handedly bridged the gap between sales and production. Loud and proud! She is one-of-a-kind. Cases of Sam Adams are always great relationship builders! Thanks T! Salespeople are like mini TV producers, they too are just trying to get their stuff on TV. They all work very hard under tough circumstances, deadlines and sometimes-unobtainable goals. It was always a pleasure working with them. Even Vowels.

CHAPTER 5

On the Road (Again)

IT ALWAYS FELT like the thirteen years I spent chasing the Grateful Dead around the country with my brother Jim prepared me for my life on the road in television. I was never a full-time traveling Deadhead catching every concert they played but managed to see one hundred thirteen shows between 1983 and 1995. That's a lot of time in the car and cheap motels, man. No regrets there! Loved every minute of it.

Pre TV travel

Traveling for television started with lots of local trips for *Front Row* and then blossomed into traveling with the Red Sox and the Bruins. Most *Front Row* road trips were within New England and were usually day trips. No heavy load there.

As that show was retooled into an hour-long documentary we started flying around the country with a little more regularity. I always considered work trips bittersweet. Bitter in the sense that it was tough leaving my wife and growing family. Time away from them was always tough, but Adrienne, as mentioned earlier, always held down the fort and I never had to worry while I was away.

The sweet part was I loved to travel. My dad was an avid traveler, and if I inherited one thing from him it was enjoying being in new places and experiencing new things. *Front Row* took us all over the US with some trips to Canada and, of course, the aforementioned Japan trip.

Traveling commercially with TV equipment is no easy assignment. There's a lot of gear to be responsible for and lots of cases. Post 9/11, traveling commercially got even tougher. I will never forget I flew from Toronto to Boston two days before 9/11 and you could simply walk on the plane. And we did because we had been running very late and were able to get on the flight with great ease. Shortly after 9/11 I recall traveling from Providence and the TSA excruciatingly going through all my audio gear claiming they'd never seen anything like that stuff before. I think I barely just made that flight!

Traveling on any assignment proved always to be a good time and always a great sense of accomplishment. There was nothing more rewarding than putting in a long day of shooting, telling someone's story and celebrating it afterward with a good meal and a couple of adult beverages. Again, camaraderie in television is very important.

A couple of memorable trips were Japan and the trip to Anderson, South Carolina, Jim Rice's hometown. Another memorable trip was for two years going to the Hockey Hall of Fame in Toronto for Ray Bourque and Cam Neely's induction. We produced programs focused around their induction and careers and the shows proved to be quite entertaining and well-made.

The weekend of Cam's induction we were invited to a private party by Bruins legend Harry Sinden. He thought it would be a good idea to show up with the camera to get some complimentary shots. Upon arriving Gara, TC, his wife Kelley and I, well dressed, decided to leave the gear in the car and just see what the party was all about. Great decision as we decided it was so small we didn't want to bring the camera and lights out at such an intimate event.

Not to name drop but Cam's friends Michael J. Fox and Dennis Leary were on hand. I had an endless glass of red wine, great appetizers and, of course, great company. We all kind of felt like we had no business being there but we were happy to be considered to attend.

In the Fall of 2002 with *Front Row* shelved, I approached Steve Sera with the idea of sending an ENG photographer on the road with the Boston Red Sox. We'd been sending the camera on the road and having a local crew member shoot pre and postgame elements and my pitch was the material coming back was uneven and inconsistent.

In the fall of 2002, I was able to ride my first Red Sox charter flight with TC, and we went to Chicago for the weekend. TC at that point, was doing fan-in-the-stands hits and a funny moment occurred when he was doing a hit with two women from Springfield. All of a sudden TC started laughing because Jerry from the booth said 'and there's a weird guy behind TC!' If the shoe fits!

Oddly enough, TC and I were at the hotel bar after the game that night when the two women we put on TV approached us. For a second, we really felt like rock stars. We thought we were being stalked. After politely chatting with them for a few minutes they abruptly left to go meet with a pitcher from the team who I can only say had aged and not well. Fact is, no one really knew if this guy's birth certificate was even legitimate.

That trip proved to be the beginning of pro-product travel time for the NESN cameramen. There was always a small NESN crew, producer, director, AP, announcers, and traveling with the teams enabled us to get from city to city faster and not get bogged down with commercial travel. Between the three full-time camera guys, Patrick Gamere and Chris DelDotto, and myself, we would look at the schedule every year for the team and decide who was going where. Eventually, with the hiring of Bryan Brennan, there were four of us in the mix traveling year-round.

Traveling with Sarah Davis

Road trips usually were either three days to two weeks long. The best part was we were not only traveling on the teams' charter but staying at the team hotel which was usually pretty darn nice. Nicer than any places I'd ever stayed before that.

Here's how the deal usually went. A game would end at Fenway and we would board a staff bus to the airport. I swear at times that bus would drive over sidewalks to get the team to the airport as quickly as possible. And always with a police escort.

Upon arriving at the airport, the bus would taxi onto the tarmac and from there we would board the plane. And the plane had everything. There was plenty of food and beverage on board. I was always proud of how my coworkers and I handled ourselves on the plane. Well, most of them! After all, we were guests of the team.

Landing in another city there would always be a bus waiting on the tarmac to take us right to the hotel. Talk about living the rock star life! Easy flight then off to a five-star hotel.

A few years later we started traveling with the Bruins as well. Same setup but they flew from a private airport outside of Boston. They used a private airline company and a private plane. Bruins trips were smaller and a little different because usually, we would get in early evening the night before the game then have morning skate the next day, play the game and then leave the city.

Baseball you would set up in the city for two to four days. The beauty of baseball was you would not have to be at the ballpark until 3 p.m. every day. That always meant you could sleep in or go explore whatever city you were in.

I'd often try to plan trips around where I had friends living throughout the US. Then of course, there were cities where you would just never leave the hotel. Detroit-why go out? Or Cleveland. St. Pete had the best bar in the big leagues. I never took traveling with these two sports teams for granted. Ever.

There were a handful of cities that I always enjoyed traveling to. New York, San Francisco, LA, Denver to name a few. Seattle and Atlanta, were also on the list.

One of the best cities on the road definitely had to be Nashville. What a great town. It's all about the music. It doesn't matter if you like country or western or neither.

Right across from the Bridgestone Arena is Broadway, almost like the Faneuil Hall of Nashville with a string of bars and restaurants. The music starts early and goes all day into the night. Bands play for a couple hours and then switch up. There's no cover charge to get into these places and if you go from bar to bar you're sure to hear some great music.

The Stage and Tootsies are the two biggies but there's a whole string of them. Not to mention Jack's Barbecue. The famed Ryman Auditorium is right there as well. There are a whole host of other great neighborhoods in Nashville, but Broadway was right near our hotel.

I was there one night with the Bruins where we had flown in from Columbus—having departed there at 11 p.m. and landing in Nashville at 11 p.m. Love those times zone changes. Knowing the next day was an off day our crew and the team took advantage of some Nashville nightlife. I'm not sure what the name of the bar was but the whole team was there and the band on stage was on fire.

The special thing about this particular band was for a $100 donation (there is that number again) you could hear them play "Free Bird" by Lynyrd Skynyrd. I believe we heard that song several times that night. The house was packed and the beers were flowing.

I must admit over the years traveling with our rink side and sideline reporters, I always took it upon myself to look after them while we were on the road. Call it a big brother type attitude but it was always important to me to make sure they were with someone who had their back. Safety in numbers.

That being said, on this particular night I was with NFR and at one point I looked up from all the excitement and couldn't find her. That made me nervous. She had stepped outside and then had come back in. OK, all was well.

As the night wore on and a few more "Free Bird" donations later I again couldn't find her. This made me rather concerned. She had decided to return to the hotel, which was no big deal. But now here I was out in front of said bar holding a parking meter up when Shawn Thornton approached me and gladly offered to walk me back to the hotel so I would return there safely. What a guy!

The next day during the teams practice Johnny Boychuck who was a defenseman with the team at the time looked up from his locker and yelled towards me, "FREEEE BIIIRD!" There the legend of Free Bird was born. Or perhaps it began a few hours earlier on Broadway.

This one right here could be the mother of all travel stories. A member of our Red Sox crew knew a guy who had a plane. They shall both remain nameless. This guy, once a season, offered to transport our crew from city to city. It was no ordinary plane, just a G4. Just enough room for seven or ten of us. Perfect.

Instead of traveling with the team we traveled in style. This trip took us from Boston to Atlanta, Atlanta to Kansas City and KC back home to Boston. I got to sit in the cockpit for our landing in KC.

There is really no other way to travel and I thought the charter was the best way. It's just you, your friends and the pilots. I've been in all kinds of small planes, but this was definitely the coolest of them all.

Again, I did not take any part of it for granted and definitely made the most of it. Pretty much the same set up as with the charter, get escorted on the runway to the plane, get on and get ready for lift off. Of course, everything was catered.

I had a great time sitting at a table with DO, Dan Aspan and Kevin Cedergren for all legs of the trips. Good times for sure!

G4 Crew

The traveling secretaries for each team were Jack, for the Red Sox, and, John Bucyk, yes, the Chief, for the Bruins. Both were top-notch professionals and I was always very impressed with the job they did. I would've liked to have had the players per diem to go along with the big-league travel lifestyle.

The unique thing about traveling with two pro sports teams is the feeling that you're somewhat embedded with the team. You are definitely on the inside. Not all the way on the inside but definitely more on the inside then Johnny from Burger King or your casual fan.

I always felt like a guest on the charters and the buses and never took it for granted. You definitely got to see a lot of these pro athletes in their natural environment that not many people ever see.

My early days traveling with the Red Sox I was told immediately to never turn around and look at what's going on behind you. That's their area. The usual set up on a plane was coaches upfront, media and support staff in the middle and players in the back.

My first few flights I have vivid recollections of a former right fielder surfing past me on dinner trays upon takeoff. There were also some players that enjoyed making animal type catcalls during takeoff. Lots of card games. Some plane rides were different than others. Obviously, after a loss, it was very quiet and usually after a win or better yet a championship win, let's just say, people were in a good mood.

I always kept it as professional as possible and definitely enjoyed being on those charters. Mostly it beat flying commercial and dealing with all my gear in airports. Bruins flights almost always guaranteed a seat next to P Dubs, never a bad thing. Always enjoyed being out there with Pat. At times, he doubled as my psychiatrist, always a great listener. 'Off Day' Pat, when he emerged, never let me down.

Patrick 'PDubs' White

From '02 on to present day there was a lot of travel. Between the two pro-product teams, away Patriot games, special projects and spring training the four of us were constantly on the road. And may I add, the success rate for the four of us was unprecedented and phenomenal. We constantly and continually performed our job at its highest level with rarely a complaint. Except of course, complaints from one particular sideline reporter every now and again!

We traveled with a producer, director, and associate producer and of course the talent. Mike 'Papi' Narracci has been the director for Red Sox baseball since early 2000. Mike and I have worked more games together than I can count. And that's just a fraction of the games that he's done. He's been calling the shots, literally, for a long, long time now and is one of the best directors in the business. How do I know? Because I worked both the home and away games with him.

I'll start by saying the Boston home show crew is the best in the business. On any telecast there is always a home show, the production of the home team in that city, and the away show, the visiting broadcast. Away, we've worked with some pretty mediocre crews. Not to say there aren't some excellent away show crews but most of the time it's a challenge and mostly for the director.

The Boston Red Sox home show, in my opinion, is the best production crew in the country. That goes for hockey as well. Both those crews consist of pretty much the same people. So many great guys/freelancers on the home show: Billy Titus; Bob 'The Godfather' Tomaselli; Clammy; Matty Johnson; Mark Wilcox; Chris Nicini; Joe Stafford; Ted LeBlanc; Kenny Boyd; Jeremy; Pete Grainger; and all the fine people in the production truck. As well as Jeff 'Crosby' Mitchell, Jim Dadano and Mike Baker.

Working with Mike Narracci challenged and brought out the best in my ability. As I quoted him in the preface, all he ever wants is an honest effort. When I was working camera on home and away shows with Mike, I always wanted to bring my best for him and for the crew I was working with.

I traveled with Mike in the Red Sox crew for over thirteen seasons. That's a lot of tbus rides, airplane rides, and time hanging out in different cities. It was always a pleasure to be working and hanging out with Mike on the road.

Like I said earlier there is a lot of camaraderie in television and Mike is a true foxhole guy. Like a handful of people that I've worked with in the business I have always considered Mike a friend first and then a work associate. And believe me that makes a big difference when you're away from home on a ten-game trip. It's good to have friends out there.

This could be the point where there are many interesting stories I could tell but I will not (there are many). All I will say is that there was no better feeling than getting on the bus after a three-game set in City X and getting that nod of approval walking past Mike that I had done my job, and hopefully, had done it well.

For the Bruins, Brian Zechello is the producer at NESN, and he was equally fun to be with on the road. Been there as long as I can remember. He had toiled on *Sports Desk* where we met when I was desiccating Master Control. I liked him immediately. He's not only funny but I saw his passion for wanting to make great television. A lot of people there had that quality but I sensed something different with Z. I would understand years later why.

Although we had different roles Z and I were very much alike in our appreciation of where we were, big picture, and how much we both loved our jobs. Brian has bridged, fostered and continues to maintain a great relationship with the Bruins. That, in turn, makes the Networks relationship a stronger one. Z is also about fun too, throughout the day and in many arenas and restaurants across the land, you can hear that laugh.

Denver

This story has to find its way into this book. Unfortunately, the guilty will be protected, but it must be told. It happened twice in Baltimore at Camden Yards approximately seven years apart from one another. On the road with the Bruins and the Red Sox, the traveling camera operator would always have to find a place to leave or store their equipment when they are away from the ballpark or hockey rink. In Baltimore, I would store my gear in the workout room directly across from the Red Sox clubhouse.

So, in year one of the story, shortly before the game and I went to put my gear away and there was one player in there working out on an exercise bike. Suddenly, he started talking to me and I knew it was to me because I was the only person in the room.

He'd started asking me questions regarding someone I worked with and how much he would like to become romantic with that person. He shared this information with me while I had my back to him the entire time. Finally, I turned around and said I believed that person was in a long-term relationship and I could not help him out. That did not stop him from waxing on and on about a potential romantic encounter that would never happen.

Fast-forward seven years later, I'm in that same room putting away my equipment and another player, a different one, begins asking me questions while I had my back to him. And believe it or not his questions also involved a potential romantic encounter with a coworker.

Before I turned around I quietly packed away the rest of my gear, stood up and walked over to the player, and told him the story of seven years earlier. We enjoyed a good laugh and I told him there was no way I could accommodate his request.

A similar not so similar story happened at Fenway Park. It was shortly before game time one night and I had to get some shots that required me to be on the field very close to game time. As I was gathering all my gear I looked down and noticed a player in the dugout who was watching me while he was eating a bowl of cereal.

Shy as I usually am, I said hello and he asked me what I was doing. I told him I was wrapping up and heading upstairs for dinner and then would be working the game. He was very polite listening and asking me different questions.

I kind of looked at him like 'hey buddy, I got to get going' and he said he had one more question for me. I said, "Okay, what is it?"

He asked me in a completely serious face, "Do you know that intern you're with and what her phone number is?"

To which I replied, "If you're that interested in getting to know my intern better, why don't you ask her yourself?"

Man, some people are shy or not so smart!

While traveling with the Red Sox in June 2016, we had a rare off day in San Francisco. Being an avid Grateful Dead fan, I took the opportunity to take a bus ride up to San Rafael and check out Phil Lesh's (famed bass player of the band) restaurant. Yes, the bus came by and I got on it.

I knew it was a good day to go as it was a beautiful Northern California spring day and I was meeting my old friend, Rick O'Hearon, for drinks and dinner. Terrapin Crossroads is the name of Phil's restaurant and just a wonderful place. It's also home of the Grate Room which is a lot like Levon Helms' barn in Woodstock, New York, a place for musicians to gather and play.

As we sat in the bar enjoying our fine tapas and craft beer, Rick tapped me on the shoulder and said, "Look behind you."

There was Phil. One of the men I had spent the last thirty-three years chasing around the country. After a few moments, I collected myself and walked over and introduced myself.

So glad I did. Phil is a true gentleman and it was a pleasure meeting and talking with him for a few minutes. Even took a selfie. I highly recommend visiting his place if you're ever in the area.

Terrapin Crossroads with Rick O'Hearon

Two places I didn't have to travel far to, were Fenway Park and TD Garden. Those places were truly my home away from home. I've probably spent more time at both those places than anywhere else during my career. Makes sense.

There was never a time when I walked down Yawkey Way, or whatever it's called now, and didn't look up at that iconic Fenway Park 1912 sign and not be appreciative that I got to work there. The Sox play eighty plus home games and the Bruins forty plus. That's a lot of nights over nineteen years including all kinds of other events.

Bummed I never shot at the old Boston Garden although I did catch fifteen Dead shows in the early 90's. Would've been pretty cool to have worked a game or two there. A building is a building, and buildings don't last forever. It's not really about the buildings but the people inside them.

I was fortunate to make many friends over the years at both places. From security personnel to ushers to grounds crew to bull gang members to clubhouse people to guys who parked cars to the people who did a lot of everything and people who did nothing at all it seemed there was always a friendly face at every turn. That's a great feeling to have at your job. How many people can actually say that?

I could pen an entire chapter on just these people alone. I do want call out a few of them. TD Garden friends: Jim and Jack McCorkle; Carlton; Tricia and Courtney; Donna Paggs; Kedo, Beatsie; and Ron the usher. Fenway Park: Donnie; Bill at the clubhouse door; Steve, the Media Dining guy; Adrienne and Katherine; Tommy; Pookie; Chris and Murph in the clubhouse; all the Joe's (young and old); Chef Ron; Bill the usher; and Chuckie the usher. Like I said, this could go on and on. All great people!

It was my pleasure to see them every day I was there. From the many early mornings and late nights, they all made the experience even better. Except maybe Steve, he was always a little rough on me.

It was not only folks like these but the entire Boston sports media contingents; TV photographers, techs, reporters, producers, and anchors. Still photographers, print media, columnists, and bloggers. I've never experienced such a loyal fraternity. Everyone in this town knows everyone else and it's pretty cool to witness and be a part of it firsthand. And for the most part, everybody likes each other.

Camaraderie in TV really spills over to camaraderie across the media spectrum. Way too many to name here. Hopefully, if you're reading this and we know each other then yes, I like you! Yes, you, too.

And one more thing. Not sure where to put this so here is good enough a place. This has to do with scrums. In TV, a scrum, by definition, is a group of people ranging from 4-40. I have been in all sizes of scrums.

The largest one was with Tom Brady when he insisted on holding his weekly media availablity at his locker as apposed to going to the podium and making it easier for everybody.

There are no rules in the scrum. Your best friend becomes your worst enemy once the scrum forms. Every person is in it for themselves.

Scrums usually consist of reporters, camera operators, writers and these days, way too many bloggers holding their cell phones.

Scrums sure have come a long way.

There is even such a thing as 'scrum surge.' It will slowly form when the player arrives at his locker and will slowly build until the player turns around and acknowledges that they are ready for greatness. Suddenly, the scrum packs around the player with everyone throwing elbows and jockeying for position.

One of the all time favorite scrums I was ever in was at Jonathan Paplebon's locker. We were all packed in like sardines. On one side I had my elbow in the sternum of the late Carl Bean. On the other side, had Tina Cervasio all pressed up against me. It was the best of times and it was the best of times. Anyone who has ever been knows what I am talking about.

CHAPTER 6

Alaska

ERIC SCHARMER HAD worked on a Cape Cod baseball documentary in 2003 with former NESN/*Front Row* producer extraordinaires Jim Carroll and Peter Frechette. I had known Eric since my early days at NESN and, as mentioned, he had always been a true mentor to me.

We developed a strong relationship early on that still thrives today. I have always respected and admired the way he goes about his business. I've learned more from Eric than anyone and a lot of those lessons were always with me on every shoot. We almost have two different styles about how we approach what we do but we have always been consistent in delivering a full effort on whatever it is we're working on.

While filming the Cape Cod documentary, they kept hearing from people—after you finish this, the next film you should focus on is a baseball league in Alaska. For anyone who is familiar with baseball, the Cape Cod Baseball League is the premier amateur summer league. Hundreds of college players have showcased their talents there for a very long time.

After the critical flop of *Summer Catch*, a film starring Freddie Prinze Jr. and Jessica Biel (although the late-night pool scene was pretty good), the league set out to find a documentary crew to tell their real and accurate story. They found Jim, Peter, and Eric. Fields of Vision (Jim and Peter's company) and Eye Candy Cinema (Eric's company) had a goal to create a series of films entitled *Touching The Game* with *Touching The Game: The Story of the Cape Cod Baseball League* being the first installment. The film was shot entirely in the summer of 2003 and was released in 2004. The film looked great and 'the powers that be' that run the Cape Cod League were very pleased.

Early in 2006, Jim and Eric approached me to join them for the last two weeks of June in Alaska to start shooting Touching the Game: Alaska. Eric had single-handedly shot the entire Cape film by himself and they were looking to add more cameras for this film, especially shooting and sequencing the baseball games.

Getting general B-roll shots for a baseball game is easy enough for one guy, but to successfully tell the story and properly sequence a baseball game more cameras are needed. I like to think I was brought along because of my baseball experience and knowledge. Who knows? Those guys may differ with me. I happily agreed and got the time off.

A project like this isn't simply just getting a group of guys together and flying out to Anchorage for a couple of weeks—it takes a lot out of planning and preparation. The fourth member of our crew was a good friend of Eric's from the Colorado days named Anthony Keel. Anthony would produce, as we all did and be the primary sound man. And boy was he good.

We rented all our gear locally in Massachusetts and went out to Alaska in the third week of June. Anthony had some friends who lived in Anchorage—Mary and Joe Von Trek. They became our Alaskan connection and to this day remain good friends of ours. Not to mention outstanding hosts and supporters of the film.

I have often said that baseball has taken me around the world. Literally. From the little league field I grew up on in Paxton, Massachusetts to Japan to the Dominican Republic to coaching thirty years in South End

Baseball in Boston, and of course crisscrossing the US covering amateur and professional baseball, this was to be the trip of a lifetime.

Alaska! Who plays baseball in Alaska? Of all places, a league in Alaska? I had many questions that needed to be answered. After all, I only really knew about the Cape Cod League, as far as summer leagues, with its prestige and history. Heck, my buddies just told its story. Of all the places baseball has brought me, I was anxiously looking forward to this one.

It was a long flight to Anchorage, but when we got there we hit the ground running. On our first full day in Anchorage, we interviewed Red Boucher who had brought the Alaskan Baseball League back to life in the early 1960s.

Red was a character and a very nice guy. He was originally from New Bedford, Massachusetts and had come into some small fame as a contestant winning the game show *Name That Tune*. His local fame led to a chance meeting with John F. Kennedy who suggested Red go west, Alaska West, and 'get involved.' So, he did.

When he got there in the early 60s he revamped the ABL that had been in a funk for a number of years. When we met Red, he was in his late eighties and had had a couple of strokes. But that certainly didn't stop or slow him down. He and his wife Vicky were gracious hosts. We shot a wonderful and enlightening interview with him and that began our Alaska Baseball journey.

A day later we were on the three-hundred-and-sixty-miles, eight-hour car ride up to Fairbanks to meet Don Dennis and the Alaskan Gold Panners of Fairbanks. What a treat. Don Dennis *is* Alaskan baseball.

Red called upon him in the late '60's and Don has been with the Panners ever since. There is nothing that he doesn't know in regards to baseball in Alaska and has had his hand in the development of the league since his arrival.

Don was happy to welcome us and we'd be staying in the famed

Olympic Village right next to the ballpark. Yes, the Olympic Village may sound like a nice place to stay to you but the OV turned out to be several trailers that were used as bunking units during the construction of the great Alaskan pipeline. Top-notch accommodations! Where's the Ritz in Cleveland now?

Not to mention it was right around the summer solstice and Fairbanks was getting close to twenty-two-hours of daylight every day. Better than the winter I suppose when there are only four hours of available daylight.

That was our lodging along with the visiting team that would be playing the Gold Panners. Lots of heavy shades to cover up the windows. It really wasn't that bad and we were very grateful that Don was hosting us.

The Olympic Village

Our first full day in Fairbanks was the summer solstice, June 21, 2006, the 100th anniversary of the first Midnight Sun baseball game ever played. The game started at 10:30 p.m. at night and was played with no artificial light. Meaning, no stadium lights for this one.

This was the first game we shot as a crew and by far our best effort. Not to take away from any of the other several games we shot over our two trips there in '06 and '07, but for some reason, we absolutely nailed this one. I was set up on the first base side and Eric was on the third base side with Jimmy manning the camera out in centerfield. Unfortunately, we left that camera's tripod plate back in Boston, so that camera was held together on a tripod literally with duct tape.

The game started and Fairbanks had its largest crowd of the year of over five thousand fans. Funny enough the next night there may have been fifty people in the stands. That's how it goes up there.

The Midnight Sun game has always been the biggest draw for the Alaskan Baseball League. The 100th game went ten innings and the home team, the Panners, won in the bottom of the 10th on an RBI single by a Taiwanese kid wearing, fittingly enough, number forty-nine.

Gold Panners? 49ers? Get it? Good. Like I said, we absolutely nailed it and it's the beginning feature which opens the film.

From that night on, we spent the next two weeks traveling around Alaska to such cities as Anchorage, Palmer and Kenai shooting with the six teams and telling many a great story. Lots of time spent either on a team bus or in the car. I wish I could say I got to see more of Alaska than I did but I didn't.

Shooting baseball anywhere the schedule pretty much remains the same on game day. Show up at the park at 2 p.m., shoot B-roll and interviews, have some dinner on the quick and then shoot the game. Although it was still light out after the game, we usually went for dinner and then got some rest for the next day.

Often times we would split up into two crews, one crew being Jim and I and the other being Eric and Anthony. They got after it a little more and were able to shoot some beautiful scenics in the wilderness but I was somewhat happy to be getting my rest when I could.

There were also many days that required us to be split up in the two crews to gather as much content as we possibly could. Eric and Anthony were a great crew and I've always enjoyed my NESN days working with Jim so we gelled great, as always!

In 2006, we were there for two weeks, and then in 2007 around the same time of year in June/July, we went back for two more weeks. This time our plan was to be in Anchorage on July 4th for a doubleheader game followed by fireworks at the end. 2007 was basically time to shoot more game footage and wrap up whatever stories we were working on in '06.

In the summer of 2007 I celebrated my 40th birthday on July 5th in Anchorage. The boys took me to dinner at the Great Alaskan Bush Company. No need to get into that tale!

Couple of great features from the film included Beau Mills, who was the son of Brad Mills, also an Alaskan league alumnus, but more notably known for being a major league baseball coach. Especially being the bench coach for the Boston Red Sox in 2004 when they won it all!

Beau was an awesome kid and story to cover. He was an up-and-coming baseball player with unlimited potential and he was great to work with. As was his dad who also was interviewed for the film.

In fact, we not only got Brad but we interviewed Terry Francona, Jacoby Ellsbury, JD Drew and several other notable Red Sox players. Former Sox PR man John Blake was instrumental in setting up those interviews. Many MLB players were interviewed as well and appeared in the film. I highly recommend it. Did I mention it's available for purchase?

Beau's professional career after his stint in the ABL did not amount to too much, I believe. I think he made it somewhat high up in the Cleveland organization, but I don't think he ever made it to the bigs. Still, he's a great kid from a great family and it was our pleasure to work with them.

Another guy we worked with and also never made it to the big leagues was a guy named Todd Sebek. Todd, a Texan, was an avid outdoorsman, a great musician and one heck of a ballplayer. We shot him fishing, we shot him playing his guitar and oh yeah, we shot him playing in a few games.

He was never really big enough and was one of those guys on the cusp of getting drafted and never did. He had all the tools needed but never got the big break that so many ballplayers hope and depend on. Hopefully, his music career has taken off as he was a very talented singer/songwriter. Knowing him and the fact he's in Texas somewhere he's probably successful.

I believe Eric and Anthony and maybe Jim made one last trip up before the film went to edit. Anthony brought a copy up for Red and on the day the film came out Red passed away. He would've been proud of our effort.

Todd Sebek at bat

We debuted the film locally at the Kendall Theatre in Cambridge, Massachusetts in 2009. It was a very proud day for the four of us. For me personally, I don't think my work had ever been on a screen bigger than a television set. The guys rented the theater to debut the film.

The Red Sox, unfortunately, were eliminated out of the playoffs the day before so we were lucky to have in attendance: Brad Mills, Terry Francona and pitching coach John Ferrell. I will never forget standing in the lobby when John and his wife walked in. John looked at me and said,

"What are you doing here?"

To which I replied, "I worked on this thing!"

I then said to John, "Oh, I guess I know why you're here," referencing the fact that they were eliminated from the playoffs the night before.

Have always liked John Ferrell from the first day I met him when he was introduced as the Red Sox pitching coach. We continued to have a cordial and professional relationship until he left the team in 2017. So nice of those guys to come and support our film. There was a question and answer segment afterward and attendance was very strong to support us.

To this day, the two trips to Alaska and the final product remain, by far, my greatest accomplishment in television. I was out in the field working with my best friends and guys I respected the most on a professional level. Unbeknownst to them, they pushed me to do the best possible job I could all the while having a great time enjoying the game we all love so much.

TIMES SQUARE ~ FMB

MARTIN GIRLS

PAPI NARRACCI

SARAH DAVIS

WINTER CLASSIC 2010

PATRICE BERGERON
2011

BISH
NFR
WALLY
WINDOW SHOPPING
'04
PARADE
PAUL
DEVLIN
THE SHOPS AT
PRUDENTIAL
CENTER
ckTours.com
DEREK
PEDRO

6.15.11

JENNY DELL
ROAD FRIENDS
JAMISON COYLE
YANKEE STADIUM
3 RBI DOUBLE
Z

DON ORSILLO
GARY STRIEWSKI
CHIEF JAY STRONGBOW

DINNER AT DONATANGELO'S
ERIC SCHARMER
ADAM PELLERIN & KATIE NOLAN
CALL OSHA

MOOSE HUNTING '07

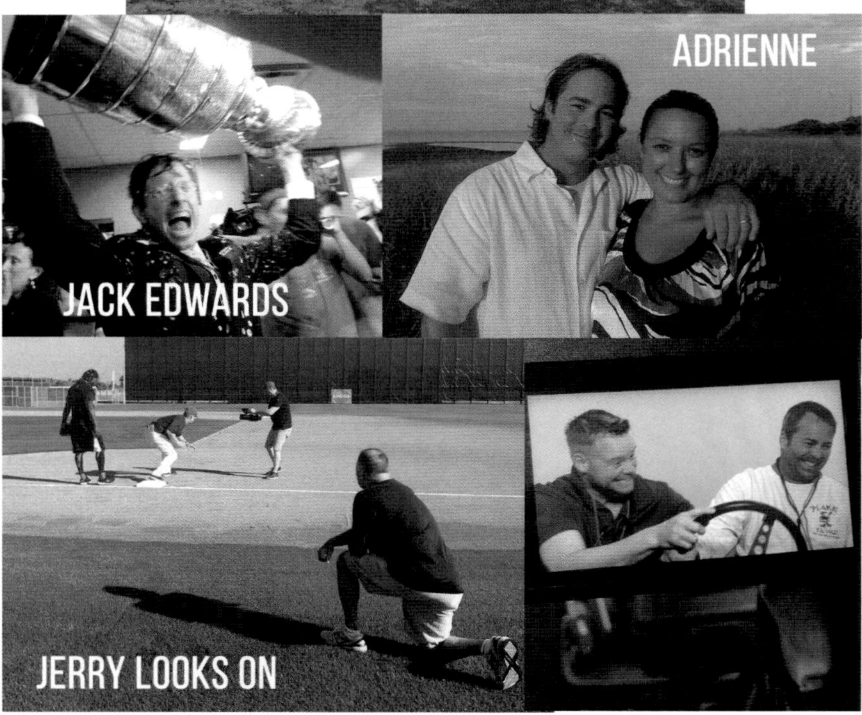
ADRIENNE
JACK EDWARDS
JERRY LOOKS ON

10.30.13

KAIA
JIMMY YO
FINAL PRESS CONFERENCE
BILL WALTON

DON CHERRY

GOLFING WITH JIM RICE
CHARLIE & BOB
GABBY
KATHERINE TAPPEN
NESN

SAM
GLASSY
WALT
ANOTHER TOUGH DAY AT WORK
EARLY FORT MYERS
JOHN CHANDLER

MY PROUDEST MOMENT
HAZEL MAE
NFR
Z
JACKMAN, MAINE
DALE ARNOLD
KAIA
BARRY PEDERSON

FORT MYERS BEACH
SADUHARA OH
STEVE GARABEDIAN
JAPAN
SARGE
LINDA COHN
ROB SIMPSON

CHARLIE & RICKY MEDLOCKE
Rickey Medlocke
BRYGUY
SHAWN THORNTON
PHIL LESH

TC
PAPI
2003
2013

SOFT HANDS
THE KING
YO
TC
VAN CREW '11

SUPER BOWL XLII
NANCY J ROSE

FMB CREW

BELFAST '10

STANLEY CUP '13

JACK & BRICK

NESN
NFR
VOLVO
F.W.WEBB
NFR
JOHN ROSS
PATRICK
GAMERE
CURACAO
KeyBank
PEPSI
CLEVELAND 2007

RED SOX
OPENING DAY '16
PRAGUE 2010
GARY & JACKIE DEMPSEY
STANLEY
NHL WINTER CLASSIC
HESS
JAMIE ERDAHL & JENNY DELL

KAIA
BIG PAPI
JEB FISHER
BOSTON
DOLPH
RED SOX
ROX
Get in the Game
PG
TINA CERVASIO
PAPI
DIANA & BILL LEE

ALASKA '06

JIM CARROLL ERIC ANTHONY KEEL

PARADISE

CHRISTINA GLENDON

CHARLIE & BOB BEERS

BOB SYLVESTER
CHARLIE
CHUCK

ELLE DUNCAN
THE TOGS
CHARLIE MOORE
HOCKEY HALL of FAME
TOM GLENNON
ALDS
'04

CHAPTER 7

Charlie Moore

CHARLIE, I TOLD that you would get your own chapter!

Where to start?

A true New England icon!

Charlie is a self-made guy. He started at NESN with thirty seconds a week and now twenty plus years later it has blossomed into the empire we all know today.

Charlie's rise at NESN was steady, beginning with thirty seconds a week on *Front Row* and eventually into getting his own show. He was assigned *Front Row* producer Bob Sylvester to produce and edit the early days of the show.

To this day Bob and Charlie are still together. They are truly like brothers. They have been through it all. From *Front Row* and its successes, the *Charlie Moore Outdoor* block was created. That was two Charlie shows and a couple other outdoor shows. The two-hour block was hosted by Charlie.

Since then he has had shows on ESPN, NBC and probably places I don't even know about, and if I'm not mistaken he's globally syndicated right now. In television that is, not the mafia.

Charlie also created his own production company called Mad Fish

Productions and he's an executive producer on a couple of Boston Bruins shows currently.

Like I said, Charlie is a self-made guy and has earned everything he's got. He even makes spices. He and his beautiful wife, Angela, have worked tirelessly behind the scenes to continue building his brand and popularity. Not to mention, Charlie is one of the most loyal friends I've ever had. He is a dedicated family man to Angela and their three kids Anthony, Nikolas, and Kaitlin. All great kids!

The first time I had been assigned to work with Charlie was in the spring of 1999 in Wolfeboro, New Hampshire. There, his tournament of champions fishing tournament was underway. My first stop on the way up was to shoot scenics of Lake Winnipesaukee from a four-seater plane, and then continue to Wolfeboro to meet up with the crew.

Well, that sounded easy enough. With a small high-eight hand held video camera, a small four-seater plane, and pilot of course, we circled Winnipesaukee three or four times. The shots I got were at best shaky, and I'm not sure if they were ever even used.

I was feeling pretty good about myself until I got back in the car and a mile later was shaking behind the steering wheel and had to pull over for twenty minutes.

I had never been in a small plane like that before and my adrenaline was so high that I just did what I could and didn't think about it until later.

Now I was late to the shoot, which one should never be in TV. There I met up with cameraman Sal Malguarnera and attempted to work the rest of the tournament but don't think I did too good a job.

You see, Mike Cole and Sal along with Eric Scharmer were the original camera guys for Charlie and they were good. No, they were great. Very big shoes to fill which took a long, long time. Charlie and Bob were patient and were happy to give me a shot.

Like I mentioned earlier, with Mike and Sal leaving the network it was now me, Patrick Gamere and Eric doing all the shooting. Patrick and I eventually got better as time went on and we understood the formula and how Bob and Charlie wanted the show to look. And we were naturally getting better as overall camera operators. There are good days and bad days when shooting a fishing or outdoor show. Lots of elements to contend with.

The one thing I've always taken pride with over the ten years that I worked with Charlie and Bob, was that we had complete creative control on how we made the show. Some of my most vivid memories are sitting at the dock at 8 o'clock in the morning with Bob and Charlie and creating on the spot what we'd be shooting that day. Most if not all the time, those two had a concept of what they wanted to try out. We did some funny, funny shit! From *Dr. Fine* to the *Bassbino* to *Survivor with Rob and Amber*—yes, them—to holiday themed shows, we did whatever we wanted, whenever we wanted.

I also have to mention the incredible amount of celebrity guests Charlie had on the show over the years. I was fortunate enough to work with Tim Wakefield, Adam Vinatieri, Adam West, Bill Lee, Darryl McDaniels from Run DMC, Bobby Orr, Barry Pederson, Chuck Clement, Gary Rossington & Ricky Medlocke from *Lynyrd Skynyrd*, Andy Brickley and many, many, many more.

Having celebrities on board was always a special treat. All of them had at some point heard about Charlie and were fishermen who really wanted to get out there and show Charlie what they were capable of. As Gary Rossington said "all the musicians want to be fishermen, and all the fishermen want to be musicians," or something like that! We always had a great time with the guests and celebrities.

Charlie & Chuck

Fishing days would usually consist of a full day of fishing with lunch on the boat and then a nice meal afterward to celebrate the great day of fishing we had. I always fully appreciated being on the boat with Charlie, Bob, our crew and whomever else we had along. So nice to shoot outdoors and like I said be our own boss.

The last show I shot and won an Emmy with Charlie was with Chuck Woolery from *Love Connection* fame. What a great day. Tough show to shoot as Chuck was chain-smoking Winston talls all day, but man was he funny. A great storyteller and definitely a must-see show.

I was very happy to win my fifth and final Emmy award with Charlie for that one. Bass Connection! Genius television.

Back to concept shows. Got to give the *Cod Father* a nod here! Bob and Charlie came up with the idea for the *Cod Father* from the *Godfather* movies themselves. Charlie of course, would be the Cod Father. Perfect casting!

We ended up shooting three different skits and we were very proud of all three. They all went something like this: somebody would piss off the Cod Father and he would somehow exact his revenge.

The three that I worked on we had a great time. It took a lot of work in regards to lighting, blocking out shots and then shooting multiple takes over and over to make it perfect. Lots of Charlie's friends and family also appeared.

Then in post-production Bob made the video black-and-white to give it that old-school texture look and feel. You'd have to see them to believe them so please log on to www.charliemoore.com right now. Lots of other great items are also there.

The Cod Father

Our trip to Curaçao still remains one of my all-time favorite weeks with Charlie and the crew. The trip was the final stop after working five days at the MLB Winter Meetings in Orlando with Tina Cervasio, and then traveling with her to the Dominican Republic for three days before going on to Curaçao.

I arrived a full day before the crew and then worked hard the next several days shooting with Doug Orr, Rusty, Bob, Charlie, Angela and our island guides. What a beautiful resort we stayed at a few miles north of the Venezuelan coast. That show had it all. Fishing, swimming with dolphins, sightseeing, even some gymnastics. I had never been that far south in my life.

Curaçao Crew

Yet another interesting story involving flying. Well, interesting to me at least. I went to a shoot on the Vermont/Canadian border in Newport, Vermont on Lake Memphremagog and Charlie had arranged with a local pilot for me to go up in his plane to circle around the small town and get shots of Charlie in his boat zooming up and down the lake. Sounds pretty straightforward . . . until I got a look at the plane.

The 'plane' was the shape of an egg with the wingspan on the top. Over the door to the egg it read 'EXPERIMENTAL' in large letters. The egg or the cockpit, if you will, was basically big enough to hold the pilot and a single passenger. I took a good long look at the plane and told Charlie I had to grab something out of the car and I would be back shortly.

By the time this book is printed marijuana will be legal in the state of Massachusetts, so I have no problem finishing this story. I went to the car and grabbed my trusty one hitter, called my wife and left her a message telling her that I loved her and our daughter and explained what I was about to do.

I then proceeded with my one-hitter in hand to the portable toilet in between my car and where the plane was docked. After a couple of blasts to the old coconut, I was ready for lift off. The effects of my visit did not fully embrace me until we were up in the air. Great timing! I figured if I'm flying around in an egg, four hundred feet above the ground, I might as well have a nice headful of something.

The cockpit was small enough that I and my camera, fit in there quite comfortably. And since there was no real door on there I was able to have a really nice view. We circled around the town of Newport about three times approximately four hundred feet up in the air.

Picture a beautiful New England town and I got some beautiful aerial shots of it. We then flew over to the lake and got even cooler shots of Charlie speeding his boat up and down the lake. We were fifty feet above the water and Charlie.

The overhead shots of him and his boat were absolutely spectacular. It also turned out to be a fun show to make as we were back-and-forth from the US into Canada, which made for some pretty funny bits. We always had fun!

Fishing with Bobby Orr. Some would say that could be an entire book. What hockey fan wouldn't want to be part of that action?! It took awhile to get him on the show but when we finally landed him it was beyond all expectations.

The special shows we always brought in a second camera and for this one we had Eric Scharmer with us. The morning started great at the dock in Falmouth when Bobby showed up with two trays of coffees and bagels for the crew. And t-shirts and hats for all. Who does that?

We headed out of Falmouth towards Gay Head on Martha's Vineyard for a day of striper fishing with Number 4—Bobby Orr! I was on the main boat and Eric was on the second boat shooting wider and prettier shots.

As usual I was up in Charlie and Bobby's mug all day. It was a perfect day and the stripers were biting, which always means a good thing in terms of a quality packed show.

Without hesitation, Bobby is no doubt the greatest athlete I ever had a chance to meet and work with. You will not meet a more humble guy. Every story that they got into on camera, Bobby would deflect attention away from him and always include anyone around him in what he was talking about. If Charlie made a reference to how great Bobby and his fellow teammates were during the Stanley Cup run in 1970, Bobby would turn it around and talk about the relationship Charlie and his crew had. We caught a ton of fish, had a bunch of laughs and everyone had the best time.

When you're out there fishing all day, by the time you come in it's usually dusk or dark, you're pretty tired but also exhilarated at the same time from all of the experiences you just encountered. The show looked tremendous especially with a lot of the pretty 'off the boat' shots that Eric contributed to the show.

Somewhere on the water

Another great fishing trip with a Bruin was when we traveled to

Kootenay Lake, in gorgeous British Columbia to fish with Hall of Famer, the Chief, Johnny Bucyk. I know it was in August 2001 because Adrienne and I had gotten married in June and our honeymoon to Bermuda was to follow that trip.

I don't recall the exact date but what I do remember is the Chief was very adamant about us arriving on a very specific day. He kept telling Charlie that's when the fish would be at their best.

Traveling to Kootenay Lake is no easy assignment. Our final destination from Boston was Spokane, Washington in the northeast corner of the state. When we met at the airport, Chief was saying goodbye to his daughter and a bunch of his grandchildren. Apparently, that's why we had to show up at that specific time—to save him all the driving between Spokane and the camp, which was well over two hours away by car.

We get out of the parking lot only to discover the Chief has driven his RV to drop them off and pick us up. What a way to travel!

We were bouncing all over that thing on the curvy, up and downs roads. We stopped in Sandstone, Idaho for lunch and then it was on to the camp. To this day, it remains one of the most beautiful places I've ever seen. The lake itself is over a hundred miles long and in some points is more than a mile wide. Absolutely breathtaking with deep, deep blue water.

We were there for three full days only so catching fish was imperative. We were blessed with the same beautiful weather for all three days, but not so much with the fish. We ended up only catching seven fish. They just weren't biting.

I felt bad for Charlie because he's a bass fisherman and those guys enjoy catching lots and lots of fish, not seven. He can fish for anything on this planet but fishing for bass is his wheelhouse.

Picture if you will, being on the boat for two and a half days, all day, and only catching seven fish.

Poor Charlie. I thought he was really going to lose his marbles. Bob was okay, a bit stressed, and for myself, I was really enjoying Chief's company, along with his friend, Walter, and the amazing scenery in front of us.

I'm sure Chief was concerned a little as well because when you bring your friends out to your fishing hole you want them to have a memorable experience, which is a shoebox of fish. Chief was a gracious host and really loved being at that camp that he's owned for many, many years.

You could tell how happy he was to have visitors. Every day we would go out with a bunch of sandwiches and cold beer not to mention amazing smoked salmon his wife had made for us. Every day we were told we had to finish everything or he would be in big trouble. I was burping smoked salmon well into my honeymoon a week later.

By the third day and only seven fish caught we decided to take it to the local golf course. Sometimes if the fishing was slow we would add an outside element to the show. Good thing Chiefs nine-hole course was right up the road. In my opinion this is where the show became legendary.

We had a golfing match between Bob and myself versus the Chief and Charlie. On one of the holes I had what was close to a fifty-foot putt—it gets longer and longer every year. When I was about to putt, Charlie grabbed the camera and 'filmed' it. Always loved that he called it filming!

The putt was a long right to left and it dropped right in the hole at Chief's feet where he tended the flagstick while adding outstanding commentary. By far, my greatest golf moment.

Charlie also captured Bob jumping all over me after I made it.

But that wasn't the end of the match because on the ninth hole Chief made a very slippery downhill putt of twelve feet to win the match. I swear he had the same look on his face when he won both his Stanley Cups.

The show ultimately turned out looking great as seven fish, some golf and some good banter between Charlie and the Chief made for a solid twenty-two minutes of television. We always pulled it off. Chief, Walter and his wife were great hosts and our journey there became yet another entry into the big book of great memories.

Kootenay Lake with the Chief

As I've mentioned before, being away from the ballpark or rink with any athlete or celebrity the vibe was always different. Granted, Johnny Bucyk played in a much different era, media wise, than say, Patrice Bergeron, with today's landscape consisting of almost around the clock coverage.

My final handful of years we would shoot the Bruins 'arrivals' at the rink game day. Year round! Bet you Chief never encountered that! But out on the water, away from it all, we got a chance to really see these guys for who they were and that was very refreshing.

On assignment with Charlie shooting in Texas with Red Sox Foxhole guy, Kevin Millar, we spent three hours once in a bathtub covered with leaves at early daybreak making duck calls to impending targets for the benefit of our show. There, you quickly learn what someone is all about. Millar had us laughing the entire time. That's what he was all about. The leaves were strictly for camouflage.

Then there was the fishing with Lynyrd Skynyrd. That show was sure a fun one to make. Who wasn't a fan of them growing up? Apparently, Charlie was, and that was enough for the rest of us to get up for the show.

It all started with a bit we shot with the band backstage when they were performing in Gilford, NH.

We did a bit with them where Charlie snuck backstage and got thrown off the tour bus while looking for the band, getting caught milling around and finally running into Ricky Medlocke, Johnny Van Zandt and their bass player. Charlie interrupted their conversation and inquired if they would be interested in going fishing. Of course, they obliged and then dissolve off to somewhere in northern Florida with Gary Rossingtons and Ricky Medlocke with Charlie. A classic TV move!

We had a scaled down crew of Bob, Charlie and myself joining the boys. We were on a plantation with those two for a couple of days. The fishing was so-so but spending time on the boat with those two with Charlie was incredible.

The first morning of fishing Gary came out with us. I can't tell you how cool it was spending the morning out on the boat with rock 'n' roll royalty! Gary, as you know, is one of the founding members of the group and he's been through it all. He couldn't have been nicer to us sharing stories of his rock 'n' roll days and his love for baseball and fishing. Plus, he caught the biggest fish of the show!

The afternoon session had Ricky joining us for a little more up-tempo in-your-face type fishing. For a man in his sixties, Ricky was a bundle of energy, and like Gary, had lots of stories to tell and it was obvious how much this guy loved fishing.

The day ended with all of us at the main cabin sharing a great meal talking about the days fishing. Again, it was one of those experiences that I made well sure that I had a full appreciation as to what was happening around me.

The next morning before everyone went their separate ways we had Gary and Ricky pull out their acoustic guitars and treat us to a medley of

Lynyrd Skynyrd classics that we taped for the end of the show.

I remember the lighting in the cabin was low, so we removed all the lampshades from the lamps to produce as much light as we could. In hindsight, I'm not sure why we didn't go outside maybe it was too cold or there was the weather. Too long ago to remember.

The final show turned out great with footage from a concert they performed at Lake Winnipesaukee, the backstage bit and of course the fishing. Truly one for the books, or should I say, this book.

Shortly after the show was cut, the band was back locally, so we met up with them and watched the show in the back of one of the tour buses for the band. They, of course, were impressed. Charlie and Bob worked their magic from beginning to end, Charlie doing a great job as host and master of ceremonies, and Bobby with a solid editing effort. Still to this day one of my favorite shows.

After *Front Row* was gassed Charlie Moore Outdoors provided the creative platform that a few of us were able to tap into over the next several years and we sure tapped into it. Outside of the concept and celebrity guest shows there are a bunch of shows just out there with Charlie and Bob only. And we had a ball, a true brotherhood.

Also had the chance to work with Matt Flanagan and Tom Glennon over the years on CMO. Nancy Rose hired us all as Master Controllers and it was great to be out of NESN on the water with those guys.

I have nothing but fond memories of my days out on the water or at Charlie's house creating the television that we wanted to make! I'm proud when I put on the television these days and see an old episode of Charlie doing his thing.

CHAPTER 8

Championship Gigs

THE LOCAL PRO sports teams in Boston have had an unquestionably amazing run in the past twenty years. I was fortunate enough to be part of a few of them, not all of them, but certainly a few special ones.

Everyone on the planet, or who is at least a baseball fan, knows about the historic run of the 2004 Boston Red Sox. Even Jimmy Dunn wrote a best seller about it.

Coming off the disappointment of the Aaron Boone home run off Tim Wakefield in the '03 playoffs everyone in the sports television business and fans alike were looking forward to the 2004 season.

We all should've known after David Ortiz hit a two-run homer over the green monster off Jarrod Washburn in Game Three of the '04 ALDS, something special was upon us! We all know what happened in the ALCS with Dave Robert's steal and the greatest comeback in baseball history with the Red Sox coming back from a 3–0 deficit to win the American League pennant over New York.

And of course how quickly the Red Sox dispatched of a very good St. Louis Cardinal team to win its first World Series in eighty-six years.

ALDS 2004

That summer was a very special one for the Martin family. We welcomed Kaia Martin on July 19, 2004, into our family and from that point on, it was very hard to concentrate on work or pretty much anything else. She was the center of our universe and my commitment to work definitely took a backseat.

So much so that when the schedule was being made for who was going to travel during the playoffs, I was informed that I would be staying home and not traveling with the team.

A programming note here: when the playoffs begin a national broadcast usually picks up the games. Meaning NESN no longer carries the games and the bigger national networks like ESPN or Fox broadcast the games. NESN's commitment at that point is generating a pre and post-game show and elements for the sports highlight show.

I was informed that I did not have 'what it took' to give my best effort in the postseason. I took that news very hard but also used it as a motivating tool during the course of the end of the season and the ALDS, and through incredible hard work, made myself worthy to be scheduled to work the ALCS and the World Series.

My thanks to Russ Kenn, our Red Sox producer, for being honest with me and challenging me to be better. And I was. Working the ALCS in the World Series with Patrick Gamere made it all the more enjoyable.

By this point, Pat and I had been working together for over five years and to work those events with him meant a lot. We worked incredibly hard and very well together. As a matter of fact, our whole crew worked really well together. Our crew consisted of Russ Kenn, Papi Narracci, Don Orsillo, Eric Frede, Patrick, Eric Scharmer and myself. At least on the road that is.

A memorable event before game one in New York found me and Eric Scharmer in NYC walking around early that morning when I stepped into a pothole off a six-inch curb into a six-inch pothole. Of course, my right ankle folded in the pothole, and I stumbled across the street and passed out on the curb. Great start!

The Red Sox were already dealing with one bad ankle with Curt Schilling, and now I was dealing with mine. It was a severe sprain that I kept wrapped and pounded Advil the entire playoffs.

At the end of game seven when the Red Sox won, Patrick Gamere and I had a very memorable time driving home from the Bronx. It was great to have that time in the car and share all those memories of what had just happened knowing we were headed to the World Series. Not bad for a kid from Brookline (PG) and a kid from Worcester (me)!

It certainly was a lot different than 2003 when I sat next to Wakefield on the plane ride home from New York after the loss.

Working in the World Series was a memorable event capped off by the Red Sox sweeping the Cardinals in four games and celebrating in St. Louis in late October. The locker room scene was unbelievable and we nailed it. At the end of the game, it was difficult waiting in the "cow line" to get into the locker room and get shots of the team celebrating, but well worth it as those shots are still used to this day.

What a great team that '04 was! Filled with all kinds of characters. Pedro, Millar, Johnny Damon, Manny, Leskanic and the list goes on and on and on. Traveling around with those guys and being on the plane with them was an incredibly memorable experience. We were happy to be out in St. Louis as Boston was raging in celebration back home.

When we landed at 6:30 a.m. in the morning after they won it all, we taxied up to the gate at the airport, where we were greeted by all the airport workers standing and applauding. That standing ovation continued the entire bus ride back to Fenway. There was a building at Roxbury Crossing that was under construction and you could see construction workers in the bare-bones building standing and applauding. There were even people standing outside their cars applauding. Goosebumps.

And then came the parade. I was fortunate enough to be the camera on the boat with the starting pitchers Pedro, Schilling, Derek Lowe, and Wakefield. Jerry Remy was on our boat, too.

The parade went from the Back Bay through downtown onto the Charles River. I have never seen so many people in my life. And so loud!

With the camera sitting on my right shoulder all the sound went up between my head and the camera and I swear I had ear damage for weeks afterward. The crowds were twenty feet deep and it was loud, loud, loud, loud for a long, long, long time.

An incredible celebration and I had a front row seat (no pun intended) on the starting pitchers boat! That turned out to be the last championship parade I ever worked. And I was okay with that. One is enough.

By the time the '07 playoffs came around, I made it a point to make myself watch more baseball. 2004 was such a blur with everything happening, I made it a point to sit down and watch the games, of course, after all my work was done preparing for the next show.

The Cleveland series was a lot of work and this time we had Tina Cervasio as our field reporter in the mix. Don Orsillo was also with us and, of course, the think tank crew of Kenn, Narracci, Patrick and myself. The best part of the playoffs was getting to work with the camera guys from our crew.

We would spend all season never seeing each other, but then in the playoffs when more than one camera was needed it was great to be teamed with them, with Pat, Bryan, Chris, and of course, Eric Scharmer filling in the gaps. Always a pleasure to be out there with those guys in the foxhole, as Kevin Millar would say. They were all foxhole guys!

The Red Sox won the World Series in Denver this time and Chris DelDotto and I were there for it. Anytime your team wins a championship it's special. My most vivid memory of Denver was we were short one hotel room so I ended up staying in Boulder with my friend Phil that proved to be a foggy good time.

The next championship gig I worked on was the Patriots in the Super Bowl in 2008 versus the New York Giants. It was very cool to work the Super Bowl. After the event, which the Patriots lost, I vowed never to work another one again.

As well produced as they are for the fans and the media it's just too long a week for any one human being, in my opinion. We were in Phoenix for an entire week leading up to the big game. Patrick, Hazel Mae, Jayme Parker, a field producer and myself. We were busy from morning till night. I'm not complaining but that's a long week.

The day of the Super Bowl our credentials would not let us into the building during the game, but somehow Patrick and I managed to get in during the first half and stuck around for Tom Petty's halftime show which was very cool.

The Patriots had a shitty game plan and did not get their act together until the second half and by that point, it was too late. David Tyree made that unbelievable catch and we all know the end of that story.

Like I said it was a very busy week shooting everything in sight in the Phoenix area. Patrick and I made sure to make the most of it and enjoy our time together. Which we did, especially at the media party.

Super Bowl XLII

The next championship I got to work was when the Celtics beat the Lakers in 2008. Again, Patrick and I were there together to share that moment. Very cool night at the garden.

I was coupled up with John Chandler and Patrick went into the locker room with Katherine Tappen to get some celebration shots. Being a Celtics fan from long ago, and actually attending the 1986 parade, it was very cool to be there the night they won it all.

KG, Ray Allen, and Paul Pierce and company did not disappoint. Also, during that run, I shot a great Doc Rivers interview in the Boston Common around the time he was hired. I always remember that interview because Doc could not have been a nicer guy and was a great fit for the Celtics while he was there. A true class act!

Onto my favorite championship, the Bruins in 2011. I was never a hockey fan until I started working at NESN, but when I left I had become a huge fan that still enjoys watching them today not to mention any other hockey game that's on.

Sorry, Owen. The Bruins have always been great to us at NESN and that 2010–2011 team was quite special.

The season began with a trip to Belfast and Prague and at midseason, hosted the outdoor Winter Classic at Fenway Park, drawing the Montréal Canadiens in the first round, and winning that series 4–3 we again knew something special was in the air.

After beating the hated Habs and advancing to Philadelphia, promise was in the air. Philadelphia proved to be a non-formidable opponent and The B's swept them 4–0.

Along this time the Fun Bunch was born. Members included Patrick, Bryan, DelDotto, Naoko, Brian Zechello, myself and a few others. For whatever reason, we were all about having fun. We worked incredibly hard, traveled a lot, enjoyed every second of it and turned out some great work! Even our announcers, Jack and Brick, were on board with us.

After Philly, it was time to take on Tampa Bay and that was another tough series. As you know, the Bruins won game seven on the Nathan Horton goal sending them to the Stanley Cup final versus Vancouver.

I did not work most of the Tampa Bay series because I was traveling with the Red Sox. My last day of the Red Sox road trip found us working a doubleheader on Sunday. This was rare because ESPN has the rights to Sunday night baseball but after two drops of rain the Red Sox Saturday Fox game was postponed till the next day. I worked eighteen innings and got home late Sunday night into Monday morning.

Monday afternoon I was on a plane to Vancouver for game one of the Stanley Cup finals. That was the first of three trips to Vancouver in a ten-day period. Patrick and I were the photographers for that series because Bryan was with the Red Sox at that point, and Chris was doing other things locally.

It was a great series with Vancouver that went seven games back-and-forth with Boston winning the last two games, in Boston and then

Vancouver. Thankfully the Bruins had complete control of game seven winning 4–0 so there was no worry on that one.

That was a great final trip to Vancouver with our crew consisting of myself, Patrick, Chris, Naoko, Rose, Jack, and Brick. I have to hand it to Jack as he was not part of the scheduled crew and got himself there on his own dime to be part of our coverage. He deserved to be there and I was so happy he was. Why he was not scheduled to be there no one will ever really know.

JUNE 2011

A cherished memory I have after they won that night occurred when we were out on the ice shooting interviews before we entered the locker room for the real party. Claude Jullien spotted Naoko and waved her over to have her meet his parents. This was not a moment for anyone to be on camera, but a truly genuine moment where Claude was proud to introduce Naoko to his parents! It was a special moment.

Inside the locker room, I immediately put a can or two of Bud Light in my pocket to celebrate with the team as I shot them celebrating. The media, especially the NESN crew, had a great relationship with the players and it was wonderful to hear Patrice Bergeron yell out my name when I walked in. I've been covering for Patrice since he was 18 and brought up with the team.

The party raged on and we got great footage and sent it all back to Boston.

Outside the arena, things were getting ugly on the streets of Vancouver as it was overrun by a bunch of suburban teens and young adults, who thought it was a good idea to smash things and attempted to burn such a beautiful city down.

The team left and we headed back to the media hotel. Our crew did not fly with the team during playoffs and we were ticketed to head out the next morning. The NHL always threw great parties for the media during the playoffs.

To think, our season began in Ireland and Prague and ended with Lord Stanley's Cup! What a great finish to a long, long season.

Like in '04 and '07 NESN gave its employees complimentary watches for the Red Sox championship victories. Many of the top brass received rings. With any championship team, there are always different levels of how nice the rings are. I always maintained my belief was that only the players and front office executives should get rings, no one else. We got nice watches and that was all well and good.

However, the Bruins made the decision, along with NESN, that everyone who worked at NESN would get a ring. The good news for the traveling party was the Bruins felt we deserved a ring a step above than what the NESN employees were getting. About fifteen of us received a very nice ring with (fake diamonds) cubic zirconia on it and our name. It's a real beauty and every time I look at it, it reminds me of what a great time that was and how hard we worked and how appreciative I was to be working with the people that I was with.

As I mentioned earlier my wife Adrienne was back home holding down the fort, now with our second child in the mix, Gabriella, who was born in November 2010. I was gone a lot of nights. Boy was she amazing doing what she did. I can never thank her enough.

2013 was an improbable championship season for the Red Sox as anyone could've imagined. They were in last place the season before and I don't think anyone thought they were going to win it all in '13. The thing is with the postseason, sometimes all you have to do is get in and anything can happen.

That year the bombing at the Boston Marathon was on everybody's mind and the city and region had come together like never before. Championships always bring a region together but this terrible event that had happened right in our backyard really brought a sense of community and togetherness.

After a thrilling ALDS with the Detroit Tigers, it was on to the World Series versus the St. Louis Cardinals again, but this time the series would begin in St. Louis with the possibility of the Red Sox clinching a World Series victory at Fenway Park. On October 30th, with David Ortiz once again the series MVP, the Red Sox won the World Series in Boston!

With our crew Patrick, Bryan, Mike Narracci, Don Orsillo, Jim Dadanno, Jenny Dell and myself our third World Series was in hand. At this point in time, we had become old hands covering postseason baseball. It was great having the opportunity to win it at home.

Boston 2013

As well as all the championship gigs I worked, I had the privilege to work a handful of All Star games during my tenure. They were exclusively MLB and NHL events. Never worked the NBA or had gone to Hawaii for the all-important Pro Bowl.

Our primary objective was to follow the Red Sox and Bruins All Stars that were selected. We would cover whatever media related events they were required to attend. We also covered any league press conferences and fan friendly events.

Usually a pretty low-key weekend from Friday to Sunday, with the All Star game itself concluding the festivities. Some cities I worked the NHL games were Montreal, Columbus. Ottawa and Nashville. The MLB found me in Cincinnati, Phoenix, KC and New York.

All memorable experiences but covering the MLB All Star at old Yankee Stadium in 2008 stands out. It was the final year of the old ballpark and a great move by MLB to host it there. My biggest early hurdle was convincing NESN that we should cover it.

The highlight show producers were a challenge sometimes, they would have us cover these random events no one ever heard about and have no interest in the sometimes more glamorous ones. Suppose it was based on budgets and such.

Anyway, I convinced them to send me alone to collect as much sound and B-roll. We booked my trip so late, I ended up at the Sox team hotel in midtown for only $734.00 a night. There goes the budget.

While in town on Saturday, I shot the All Star parade. All the players were in the back of pickup trucks waving to their adoring fans. The best part of the entire weekend was working alone. I could go anywhere when and for how long I wanted. Complete creative control. The game itself became the story though. It was a fifteen-inning marathon clocking in at four hours fifty minutes. J.D. Drew received the MVP award for tying the game in the seventh inning although I would've given it to Michael Young of Texas for winning it in the fifteenth. Thanks to Dan Roche for sticking it out as long as I did and holding my microphone at two in the morning.

CHAPTER 9

The Fort

FORT MYERS, FLORIDA. The City of Palms. Tucked away in beautiful Southwest Florida. The ol' RSW. Home of the pelican person and the spring training home of your Boston Red Sox. Also, home to seventy-seven thousand plus residents. Shouldn't forget them I suppose. By definition a pelican person is usually male between the ages of thirty and sixty, very tan, usually wearing old dirty white hightop sneakers, cutoff shorts with no shirt and usually chain-smoking. They can usually be found at any bus stop. That's a pretty accurate description.

Fort Myers itself has been a spring training destination for many teams over time. Terry Park hosted the Philadelphia Athletics from 1925 to 1936. The Cleveland Indians were in town in 1941 and 1942. The city's next residents were the Pittsburgh Pirates in 1955 through 1968. Roberto Clemente was part of those Pittsburgh teams. The Pirates left after 1968, but Fort Myers and Terry Park did not remain empty for long as the Kansas City Royals came to town in 1969 and stayed through 1987. In 1991 the Minnesota twins made Fort Myers its spring training home and are still there. The Red Sox moved to Fort Myers in 1993 from Winterhaven, Florida.

A lot of facts, I know. But when you're the self-proclaimed Mayor of

Fort Myers you need to know these things. As of July of 2018, Randall P. Henderson may still be the official mayor but we all know who the real mayor still is. No offense RH! Only Lois Thome of WINK News may have more power than both of us.

I began covering Red Sox spring training in 2000. Fort Myers has also been described as 'Anytown USA' by some, meaning there are long stretches of road with nothing but every imaginable restaurant and store you could ever think of. There are very few neighborhoods and downtown actually has some character to it. All in all it's actually a very nice place that's steadily been growing for years.

When I began covering spring training NESN's commitment was only two weeks out of the six plus weeks that the team was there. Like most stations, we would go down at the very beginning to gather as many interviews and B-roll as possible and then return once the spring training games themselves had started which was usually around week four.

The first couple of years I went there should be considered part of the dark ages of television. We would shoot all day and then rush our beta tapes to the airport and put them on Delta for the flight back to Boston. Delta Dash it was called. We would have to get the tapes on the plane by 4:30 p.m. and they would arrive in Boston usually around 9:00 or 10 p.m. I recall a pair of Pedro Martinez and Nomar Garciaparra interviews not making it back to Boston because of weather (snow) or missing the connection in Atlanta.

I made one trip to spring training in the year 2000. Pretty benign and got my feet wet for the first time. In 2001, my first trip was innocent enough, down and back, and we got everything we needed. Before the second scheduled trip to the Fort, I was out in Las Vegas covering the John Ruiz/Evander Holyfield fight and could not make it back to Boston, again due to weather.

At the Vegas airport, I finagled a flight to Fort Lauderdale and then had my sister, Denise, and brother-in-law Don come over from Naples to pick me up and then drive me over from the East Coast back to Fort Myers. That was one long day of travel! 2001 proved to be a very important year in Fort Myers to me because of one small place.

Fort Myers Beach (FMB) is a very small stretch of beach southwest of Fort Myers on Estero Island. It only took one trip there to discover two very special places, the Top of the Mast bar and Plaka, a Greek restaurant. Two very nondescript places but two that I frequented often for years to come.

My inaugural trip there was with producer Bob Leone and we were later joined that night by Don Orsillo. It was love at first sight for me. A dive bar with picnic tables right on the beach with a perfect view of the daily sunset. Many would ask me over the years, have you been to Sanibel, Captiva, anywhere else? There was nowhere else as I had discovered my perfect paradise.

Here's a typical trip to Fort Myers Beach: plead with my coworkers to make the forty-minute drive over the bridge sometimes in long traffic. Then park in front of the Top of the Mast, hit the beach around 4 p.m. for much frisbee and swimming.

The Mast was also home of a famed rumrunner drink, which came in a snazzy souvenir glass. Many of my work colleagues to this day own many glasses. I personally own at least ten at the moment. I know Gara has a bunch.

After a couple of rumrunners and watching a glorious Southwest Florida sunset, we would then move over to Plaka for a great Greek meal. Being a big fan of the chicken kebab platter, it became the only entree I ordered for fifteen years.

The real beauty that FMB offered was a relief from 'Anytown USA' and the ballpark. You can get pretty crusty covering spring training all day, going back to the hotel/showering and then going out to dinner. Repeat day after day after day.

The beach represented a great getaway—almost a place to cleanse oneself. I chartered countless trips to the beach over the years and anyone who was ever on one would tell you it was well worth it.

My wife Adrienne, who had already been joining me for short trips at spring training, brought our daughters down every year. We have many great family memories with our girls there. In fact, after I had retired our first trip was to stay on the beach at Fort Myers Beach.

FMB was also the place where the mystique and legend of the Blue Dolphin was born. It was a typical year for our friend Dolph who was getting his annual butt kicking from the lads back at 480.

After getting him down to the beach one afternoon he discovered a pod of dolphins heading east to west in the water toward the setting sun. He followed those dolphins and when he returned hours later he was changed. Changed in the most positive way a human being could be. These were/are beautiful mystical creatures and he was drawn to them quickly and soon we all were.

You see, Blue Dolphin is not an animal or person but rather a state of mind, a state of wellbeing, a state of calmness. This may be a lot for a regular or simple-minded person to comprehend but for our group we were all on board.

That's pretty much all you need to know about Fort Meyers Beach. Top of the Mast, Plaka and the Legend of Blue Dolphin. In the two spring trainings I have not covered since retiring, I was very pleased to get pictures and posts from friends at FMB which made me very proud. Almost like I started something. Again, the Mayor hard at work!

Top of the Mast

While the Sox were at City of Palms Park in the early 2000's, Don Orsillo and I were trying to land an interview with controversial player, Carl Everett. Carl had run into a bit of trouble with umpire Ron Kulpa the season before on a close play at first base, which resulted in Carl being ejected from the game. Carl was a pretty far out dude to begin with, not believing in dinosaurs or the idea that man had walked on the moon.

I was confident that we were going to get an interview with him. One night at the Fort Myers Ale House, an establishment where media folks and ballplayers alike would patronize I saw Carl and realized this was my chance to see if he could be available to sit with us. I approached him and kept talking about how we could sit him down and talk about all things except umpires and dinosaurs and would he be available the next day? I just kept talking!

He agreed and the look of disbelief on Don's face when I told him whom we'd be interviewing the next day was priceless. The next day arrived and out of courtesy, I told then Sox PR man, Kevin Shea, that we were going to be sitting Carl down for an interview.

Kevin took one look at me shook his head and said, 'You'll never get Carl."

When that word Carl was coming out of his mouth, here came Carl himself from the clubhouse and looked at me and said, "Are you guys ready?'

I said you bet and we brought Carl out for a quick ten-minute interview.

I told Donnie to keep it all about his workouts and spring training and if things were going well towards the end of the interview ask him finally, "Carl, are you misunderstood?"

That soundbite we got from him lasted over ten minutes and made for some great television.

Carl was later on the Charlie Moore show, with Eric Scharmer shooting, and apparently, he spent a good portion of the afternoon farting off the back of the boat! Classy.

Kevin Shea would later be involved in another situation that would actually cost me a good sum of money.

Pedro Martinez's girlfriend was with him at spring training and she was an aspiring on-air reporter type. Pedro had approached me and asked me if I was free for a day to shoot her doing a bunch of mock type interviews.

I said sure, as I was excited about the opportunity to work away from the ballpark with Pedro. When he asked me, there was never any discussion of money. I was just happy to do it.

Then Kevin stepped in and kiboshed the shoot, stating as a NESN employee I was too close to the players and it wouldn't be appropriate.

The gig was handed off to Pablo Cortez of Channel 7. It was a full day shoot with multiple takes. Luckily Pablo is a very patient guy and was happy to do it.

A few days after the shoot, I was in the dugout at City of Palms Park talking with Pablo when Pedro walked out and asked if he could talk to Pablo real quick. Pablo obliged and when he came back he was a thousand dollars richer. That one stung!

2003 welcomed new management to the Red Sox and a larger commitment from NESN in regards to our spring training coverage. Prior to traveling to Florida that year, I was told "pack for ten days or six weeks—we are not sure yet."

Well, I ended up staying six weeks missing out on a Charlie Moore outdoor shoot in the Bahamas with Harry Sinden. Oh well.

Halfway through the trip I got a call from upper management at NESN asking if they could send my wife down for a week or so and they'd pay for it. How very nice.

Funny, while I was on the call there happened to be a loudspeaker above my head and suddenly it boomed, "Martin, party of one to the first tee." I happen to be at the Fort Myers Country Club getting in a quick nine holes when I got the call.

Years came and went and I enjoyed every spring training I worked. No shocking news there, I loved to cover spring training. What's not to like or love? There was baseball, sunshine, a break from the cold weather back north and the fact that my wife and growing family were coming down to visit every year.

Even my good buddy Matt Hanley put a real nice run of years together coming down from Atlanta.

Duties at spring training ranged from covering the team day to day, to shooting all access features, to working with our creative services department shooting commercials. Just about anything that had to do with the Red Sox, we were available pretty much day or night.

There was one spring training a producer I will definitely not name (Pat Cavanaugh), who made it a point to have me cover every spring training game while I was in Florida. That meant Fort Myers one day, Jupiter Florida the next day, Tampa Bay the next, shooting every inning and every player—just in case somebody did something of significance. What a colossal waste of time. He didn't last long at the network. In fact, he also wrote in one of my annual reviews that I referred to John Henry face to face as " Dude."

Now, I'm not the smartest guy in the room, and I've called a lot of people a lot of things, but I never called the principal owner of the Boston Red Sox *Dude*. Seriously dude!

In 2012, the Red Sox moved into JetBlue Park after several years at City of Palms Park and traveling the three miles up and down Edison Avenue to the Players Development Complex. It was really the opposite way you wanted your spring training complex to be structured and the team became tired of trying to sell the illusion that riding up and down Edison Avenue in the trolley car was fun.

It simply was not functional. Edison Avenue ran through a pretty bad part of town. Glad to have befriended Todd Stephenson before the Sox moved south of town. He's a real good friend regardless of what TC says about him.

The Red Sox built a beautiful complex on Daniels Parkway just east of Route 75. The main ballpark, which is an exact footprint dimension-wise as Fenway Park is the main jewel and on the other side of the green monster are six practice fields. This place has it all, a state of the art facility. I loved going there every day and wish I'd had one of those Fitbit bracelets while I was working because I walked more miles than I ever could have imagined.

The best part was knowing that you are driving to one place for the whole day and not three miles up and down a road from one facility to another. From 2012 to my last spring training in 2016, I made many friends at the JetBlue complex. Anyone will tell you I'm not shy and will talk to pretty much anyone. I became good buddies with a number of the security guards there and for years tried to talk Dan Ricci into signing me to a contract after my retirement.

I figured I should sign something now because they'd all be gone by the time I retired. Little did I know I'd retire before all of them.

JetBlue Park

Guys, like my two good buddies, Bob Maloof and John Falcone. Tom Frost, Tom Delaney, Izzy, John Ruzanski, Kevin Clapp and Jay Fandel were all folks I enjoyed seeing every day while I was down there. It was always fun to shoot the breeze with them as they were enjoying a nice retirement gig and I was enjoying just being at spring training and in The Fort.

Funny, as I write this chapter the Red Sox are winding up their 2018 spring training playing an exhibition game against the Chicago Cubs from JetBlue Park. Man, what I'd give to be there right now. Did I mention how much I loved spring training?

As I briefly mentioned earlier, of all the duties we had at spring training, one of my more favorite things to shoot was the All Access show we produced. The premise of the show was to spend the day with a Red Sox player from morning till night. It really turned out we spent time with them from morning till whatever time they decided to go home in the mid to late afternoon. The segments ran from four to six minutes long, and I found them to be quite enjoyable.

The first year, Jeb Fisher and I worked on the project and in the following years Steve Garabedian and I shot them. In 2013 Jeb and I began the show with a great segment with David Ross. Another really enjoyable segment was with pitcher Jake Peavy. Both Jeb and I or Steve and I would operate a camera to maximize the amount of video we collected.

Although one year some clown assigned another clown named Ryan from Minnesota to join our crew to get 'specialty shots.' He was touted as a 'reality show specialist.' Wonder if he worked for the current president? What a buffoon!

That kid spent more time in the way and overcompensating for nothing and he just became a royal pain in the ass. The capper was one night he ordered a cosmopolitan drink (no offense to Cosmo drinkers—I like them, too) at a barbecue joint. Who does that?

Jeb and I had a good laugh about that one. Cosmo-daddy! What a dink. But I digress.

The features were well shot, well edited (thanks Kevin Newton) and were well received! Just like the *Front Row* Days.

The Fort will always hold a special place in my heart.

CHAPTER 10

In Others' Words

I'VE REALIZED THAT writing a book can be a tiring laborious effort. Sort of. So why not let some of my esteemed colleagues do the job. The following are a collection of tales involving your humble wordsmith told for someone else's POV. Enjoy.

With John, it's never work. It is more about transcending the work and finding a greater meaning behind the work, and most importantly, being in the moment. There are truly too many examples for me to recount, too many lessons and too many very deep conversations . . .

Here are a few Kodak moments . . .

It's 2003, and we are sitting literally on the stairs in the aisle as the Red Sox clinch a playoff berth for the first time in years. The crowd has more energy than we can ever remember, and John says "it's happening." It was the exact kickoff to the Red Sox breaking the curse in 2004 and he knew it.

It's 2005, and we are sent to Arizona in spring training to sit down every team that the Red Sox will face in the upcoming season. John could clearly see that I was scared to death to approach Greg Maddux, Nomar Garciaparra, Carl Everett . . . to which he sat me down and said "just be

Winnie the Pooh. . . . Winnie likes honey . . . he eats it . . . Winnie just is . . . You want interviews . . . you just are."

It's November of 2007, and me, John and Tina Cervasio are sent to Jackman, Maine to go moose hunting with Jonathan Papelbon. The three of us are caught in a flash flood from 3 a.m. to 7 a.m. The headlights of our SUV were fully submerged in water, no cell phones, spitting snowflakes. Very tense and very little conversation. John said, "ya know . . . they'll never find my body. They'll find you guys, you're the on-air talent and producer . . . but they won't search long for the 'tog"

It's a stretch from 2007 to 2013 where spring training in Fort Myers, Florida was not about the unsurmountable production challenges we faced . . . and more about what as John coined "The Fort" was trying to tell us. We would arrive every day before sunrise just so John could shoot the sunrise each morning thru the sprinklers because John knew it was "art" that the shows needed and, more importantly, we needed it

It's raining. "The Fort is very unhappy with us."

A mechanical problem. "She's trying to tell us something. There's a lesson here."

A dolphin emerges from the ocean. "She's giving back to us."

It's ten years of shows where John would roam ballparks, looking for that art that would be perfect for the show. The art that was more important than the game and more fun grabbing fans, hot dog vendors, painters, cheerleaders anyone that would show how great being in the moment is!

~Mike Barry

In the Summer of 2007, John Martin and I headed to Southern California to bang out an episode of *Rubber Biscuit*, a delightful little half-hour TV show that NESN utilized to support its Boston Bruins game programming.

I was the host and co-producer and John was the videographer or "shooter." NESN staff producer, Steve Garabedian, was along as well to offer whatever assistance he could and to make sure we stayed out of trouble. We'd take part in an activity with one of the Bruins near the player's off-season home, profile his on-ice performance over the years, incorporate a travelogue of some sort in the local area, and produce another story or "package" about that player or someone else in the NHL.

In the case of SoCal, we were visiting veteran Glenn "Muzz" Murray in Manhattan Beach. As part of the show, he and I, and his former Los Angeles teammate, and sort-of neighbor, Rob Blake, the Captain of the Kings, went surfing, longboarding to be exact. Longboards are much larger and thicker than the typical surfboards you see in the crazy big wave highlight videos or movies.

They're called "tanks" amongst surfers and offer an easier ride. Muzz and Blake were pretty good, while I hadn't ridden one since I lived in Hawaii eleven years earlier.

John got some amazing shots of the boys doing their thing, some dolphins frolicking on the surface behind us, and of other Californians tearing up some bigger waves on shorter boards. He also somehow got a cool transition-to-commercial shot of the title *Rubber Biscuit* written in the sand and being erased by an encroaching wave. Not sure how long this took him or how many tries, but even with a tripod locked in position holding the camera, nailing the timing of it couldn't have been easy. That would have been a spot where Gara helped out.

Another little transition we always used to get for each episode was a tease and a toss with a hot chick or two. Throw political correctness out the window, whether it was a Boston Bruins "ice girl," a woman on the street, or in this case, a bikini-clad beachgoer, we would always do our best to find the best, cutest, and brightest to spice up a toss or two to commercial breaks. Things like, "Hi, I'm Tawny, you're watching my favorite show *Rubber Biscuit*, and we'll be back right after this."

The SoCal beach was very likely our favorite ever locale for securing these random little "throws" to break.

We found Alex in a white, flowered bikini. She was beautiful, well spoken, and executed the little "bump to break" just perfectly.

While walking around looking for our second starlet, we came across a classic old-school greasy tanned guy. This dude was in his mid-forties, with a mustache from the 1970's, was absolutely greased up with tanning oil from head to toe with leathery brown skin. Naturally, he wanted us to put him on TV. That wasn't happening, but he did follow us around on our quest for a few minutes, which led to one of the funniest/coolest lines in *Rubber Biscuit* history.

We stumbled across Morgan, a beach babe through and through in a red bikini. She was "like oh my God, right on, so cool." We handed her the NESN mic and told her what lines to repeat. "Hi, I'm Morgan from Palm Vista, California, and you're watching *Rubber Biscuit*. Please stay with us, we'll be right back."

But before she started, while holding the mic and getting ready to speak, she said "alright, alright, alright" which in her voice came out "al-rah, alrah, alrah", then she noticed leather tan guy standing next to us, looked over in disbelief, and blurted out, "Dude, how'd you get that tan?!"

We used this little outtake as the last thing seen at the end of the show.

We had a delightful time with this production and when the gathering of materials was concluded, John, Gara and I hopped on a plane for Minnesota to do it all over again with Bruins Andrew Alberts and Brandon Bochenski. I'd have the Cali show written by the time we landed.

Minny meant more good dudes, more fun content, and more relaxed creativity. "Motty," with a jokingly heavy Boston accent, was how I referred to Martin when I wasn't simply calling him "Marty". We were born to work together. No muss, no fuss, need this, get that, thanks for coming. We shared lots of laughs during our many travels but never lost sight of the prize: the content. Executed efficiently with respect.

Rubber Biscuit seemed to be a cult favorite in a way. People were drawn to its quirky nature, it was fast paced for a "magazine show," and some fans, media, and players still bring it up to me more than a decade later. I truly believe it's the people who worked on the episodes as the crew; shooter Pat Gamere, shooter Chris Deldotto, producer Sarge Kerrisey, editor Kevin Newton, Gara, and of course Marty, who conveyed their personalities, approach and attitude through the programming. The atmosphere behind the camera was displayed in front of it, which made it extremely likable.

In reflecting on this I only can think of one way to express a conclusion: Thank you very much, my dear friends, for an unforgettable experience.

~Rob Simpson

You Are The Papi

Dateline circa 2003

John, Russ Kenn, Eric Frede, and I took a gypsy cab from Yankee Stadium to Midtown following a Red Sox/Yankees marathon. I was in the front passenger seat, John, Russ, and Eric were in the back. The driver was a very nice Dominican guy. When he found out we were with the Red Sox, he was very excited and only wanted to talk about Manny and David. Somewhere in the conversation, John decided to tell everyone about how much Adrienne liked Mark Belhorn.

Out of the corner of my eye, I can see the driver becoming agitated. The more John embellished her attraction to Mark, the more he became silently agitated. Finally, he could take no more of this talk, and decided he needed to lecture John about the dynamics of husband and wife. He summed the lecture up with a very emphatic "You are the Papi!"

Flash forward one year . . .

John, Russ, Eric and I jump into a gypsy cab from Yankee Stadium following yet another Red Sox/Yankees marathon. Same seating arrangement, SAME DRIVER! I spend the first few miles of the trip looking in the rearview mirror trying to make eye contact with John. We finally make eye contact, and now I have to communicate to him that we are with the same guy.

Like a couple of twelve-year-olds, we start silently communicating with lip reading and facial expressions when it finally kicks in.

Of course, John, who talks to everyone, reminds the guy of the story from a year ago. The guy sort of does a double take looking at John, and when John summed it up by reminding him "you told me 'I am the Papi,'" there was instant recognition in his eyes.

We all had a good laugh and John and I, among others have called each other "Papi" since that day.

~ Papi Narracci

I have known and been friends with John for almost twenty years and have been around the U.S. and Canada with him on many shoots. As others have probably stated, John is one of the all-time greats to travel with, as he makes working a breeze, and will laugh and joke with anyone.

During the two summers filming in the land of the Midnight Sun while making *Touching the Game: Alaska*, we were pretty much guaranteed an interesting and unique experience every day. The people we met and the stories we heard could fill a book by itself.

Often times, our four-man crew (John, Eric Scharmer, Anthony Keel, and myself) would split into two groups to film. On one sunny day in Fairbanks, Eric and Anthony would head to fish with a couple ballplayers, while John and I traveled to the town of North Pole, Alaska, home of the now defunct North Pole Nicks baseball team.

North Pole, Alaska, is about ten miles outside of Fairbanks. The town was founded in the mid-20th century, and soon after adopted the Christmas theme. It remains a tourist attraction today, complete with a Santa Claus house, and post office, although besides a couple of oil refineries there is not much more to North Pole.

The Nicks played in the Alaska Baseball League during the league's heyday in the 1980s. They had Santa logos and wore candy cane striped uniforms. Our goal for the day was to not only film a little of the touristy stuff, but to locate Wright Field where the Nicks once played, and interview John Lohrke, the Nicks former general manager. John Lohrke is the son of former major-leaguer Jack "Lucky" Lohrke who escaped death several times and later played on the Bobby Thompson NY Giants teams of the early 1950s.

You may have a wintery vision of us filming in North Pole, Alaska, but on this eighty-degree day we were rocking shorts and T-shirts. After filming the world's largest fiberglass Santa statue, we arrived at Wright Field. It was now overgrown and in need of repair. We set up and interviewed Lohrke who spoke of the great Nicks players of the past such as Mark Grace, Luis Gonzalez, and Todd Zeile.

He also gave us a few legendary "Only in Alaska" stories that we had now come to expect (yes—after a rainstorm, they used to dry Wright Field by pouring gasoline and setting it on fire). After the interview, JPM went to film some more field scenics, as well as some of his patented "The Gods of Baseball are looking on" shots.

Well, the baseball gods must have been on a break, because suddenly I hear a crazy blood-curdling scream, followed by JPM sprinting out of one of the dugouts. While filming, John had stumbled upon a wasp nest, and they were out for a piece of our famous, fearless cameraman.

I'm not sure how many stings he received but it was nothing a drive-thru Wendy's and a beer or two couldn't heal.

I still have the recording of John's scream somewhere. Quite a day at the North Pole.

~ Jim Carroll

TRUNK SLAMMER

I talked with James Driscoll the other day. First time we'd connected since he'd played in the 2001 Northeast Amateur golf tournament at Wannamoisett Country Club in Rhode Island.

He'd been twenty-two years old at the time, a recent graduate of the University of Virginia who'd been prominent on the New England golf scene since he won the club championship at Charles River CC in Newton when he was only fourteen years old.

James was what you might call a "golf prodigy" back in the early '90s although in our conversation I think he might've preferred I find another way of describing his prominence in the game back then, but, trust me, he was prominent. Both regionally in New England while having "had some success on the national level of junior golf" as he described it.

John Martin, Eric Scharmer and I were at Wannamoisett in June of 2001 for a story on Driscoll's play in what he recalled recently as being his "favorite tournament . . . ever" to play in back in his days as an amateur. Ben Crenshaw had won there, so had Dustin Johnson, David Duval, Notah Begay III and some others whose names are easily identifiable with the game at the highest level.

We were there to chronicle this particular event in the golf career of a young man who gave signs of being the next New Englander to accomplish prominence at the PGA level. I mean only a couple of months earlier before he'd even graduated from college he shot a 68 in the first round of the Masters at Augusta where his playing partner, Tom Watson, called it the best round he'd seen by an amateur.

So, the three of us saw the assignment for NESN's *Front Row* as potentially a piece of golf history as we tracked Driscoll in what he called "maybe the best stroke play amateur tournament in the country."

He told us "it felt like a home game in a lot of ways." We kinda thought and hoped he might choose this venue to make it official that he was turning pro. If he had it would've given our story some legitimate news value. I tried. I asked the question. He ducked. Oh well.

It was a beautiful day. John and Eric did their video magic and as reporter/producer, I did my best to appear to know what I was doing. James didn't win. We, of course, were hoping he would cuz that, too, would've given the story some whack. He shot rounds of 69, 76, 71 and 65 and tied for 17th.

Luke Donald won it for the second straight year. We were there for the 65. Hell of a round! Truth be told in the spring of 2018 none of us have a single clear recollection of anything about it. Neither does Driscoll.

It was a weekend. What we'd shot wasn't to be edited that day and there was no rush to get back to NESN's Fenway Park location. No rush. We packed up and on I-95 heading north, we saw the billboard touting Stone E Lea, a little public golf course in Attleboro MA coming up at the next exit.

Sumbitch!

Why not?

So, we did.

Our round at Stone E Lea was comparable to Driscoll's 65 on his final round at Wannamoisett in one way. None of us today have a single clear recollection of anything about it. Just three bozo buds hooking, slicing, chunking, splashing, giggling and cussing around a golf course that had jumped in front of us on the drive home. Scharmer was probably okay. He usually was. I'm sure I sucked. Typical. And John had what Driscoll described in our phone conversation a few days ago as "a trunk slammer." It's a phrase common among golf pros who miss the cut, toss their clubs into the back of the car and?

"Trunk Slammer."

Y'know?

What *is* memorable about Stone E Lea, and we all remember it clearly, John Martin didn't slam the trunk. Nor did he put his fist through a wall in the restroom or toss his putter into a pond as now golf pro James Driscoll will acknowledge he has done.

He did, however, pull off the Martin equivalent. In the parking lot, a woman had just gotten out of her car three or four parking spaces away. John picked up his golf bag and with no anger, in fact, with what I recall as a contented smile, then with profound calm, politely gifted her his golf clubs. Very few words were exchanged. She was amused, perhaps bemused, and as I recall, slightly confused as well. John thanked her and she him. He came back to the car wearing the same contented smile and we left.

That . . . we all remember.

Only John!

~Lanny Lee Larason (formerly Tom Larson)

ONE STEP FORWARD ANOTHER STEP BACK

Just about fifty weeks after Grady Little suffered a monumental brain cramp managing the Red Sox ALCS Game #7, which led to an Arron Boone walk off home run sending the Yankees to the 2003 World Series, John Martin and I were in New York for Game #1 of the 2004 ALCS.

I was a call to the bullpen and drove down from Boston without a hotel room the night before only to crash on a rollaway in JPM's room.

The morning of Game One, I'd planned to walk a dozen blocks or so to a big camera shop in midtown to purchase a new camera for my business, and Johnny was happy to get out of the hotel to get things going.

The morning of big games it's not at all unusual to start getting jacked up about how the day's events may unfold. As a photographer no matter the outcome, you know that in a situation like Sox vs. Yanks battling to go to the World Series, the postgame locker room is going to be a war zone due to the volume of media wanting player sound.

Whatever adrenaline may have been running through us at 8:00 a.m. upon waking, we still needed coffee, that was sure. We bounced down to the lobby, and if I'm not mistaken had a few exchanges with Red Sox personnel, because that was what Johnny did, always a people person.

As we hit the crowded sidewalk and headed south we were packed in shoulder to shoulder amongst fans of the Evil Empire, and I'm sure that we were both proudly wearing Red Sox hats just hoping someone would recognize the red B's and want to start some rude banter, cause John Martin and I were ready to throw down . . . with words anyway.

So much going on around us on a Manhattan sidewalk it was easy to get distracted. Yankee fans giving us the evil eye, the tall buildings surrounded by equally tall women, the sights, sounds, smells all taking a toll on our sensory overload and we hadn't even gotten coffee yet.

I must admit that I do believe we were jaywalking when we went to spring through an intersection with the big orange hand illuminating solid from the pedestrian signal. We stepped off what was an unusually high sidewalk curb which seemed like it must have been close to ten inches above the asphalt below, but only John stepped into a canyon of a pothole throwing him face and chest first into the street in front of a rapidly approaching taxi.

It's this part of the story where I typically take vast amounts of credit for pulling Johnny out from in front of the speeding yellow taxi, driven by some guy with a Yankees hat ready to squash the fallen kid in his path from Beantown.

Looking back, I can't help but be reminded of a line from the movie *Crocodile Dundee*, "Ain't no crocodiles in Manhattan but a fast movin' Chevy will sure make a mess of ya."

Happily, John P. Martin was saved!!!!

Yeah, he was saved, however looking down at his immediately swollen ankle, knowing what a physical job shooting Game One would be, knowing all that he was responsible for, and the people who were depending upon him, he may have opted for the fast moving Chevy.

JPM picked himself up and hobbled back to the hotel in hopes of finding a member of the Red Sox medical staff to help him with his situation as he had no intention of being placed on the DL, not tonight.

As it turns out both John Martin and the Red Sox limped back to Boston having dropped both ALCS games in NYC, and the pain persisted in ALCS Game Three as the Sox got torn up at home.

Then as the true healing began for Red Sox fans across the globe with Dave Roberts about to steal second base keeping the dream alive, so did John Martin heal on the front lines while capturing historic moments through his lens for Sox Nation in 2004.

When it was all said and done, Johnny played through the pain during the ALCS and the World Series, only to hit pavement once more outside Fenway Park as we both stepped off our respective duck boats after documenting the Sox MLB Championship parade which was the final act of a story eighty-six years in the making.

~ Eric Scharmer

March 3, 2000.

Do you know where you were that day? I do.

In all our years working together only once did John and I drive into a town that had a "Welcome NESN" banner hanging in the center of town (it was written on an old bed sheet).

The town: Berlin, New Hampshire.

The story: 24 hours of broomball (if you're not familiar with the sport, google it).

We got to the arena and right away John started shooting B-roll, while I sat in the stands watching. Sitting in front of me were two women who I overheard talking about the cute cameraman shooting the action. I laughed and they turned around. I told them I was working with him and his name is John. One of them then said to me "He's gay right?"

I couldn't stop laughing, but I told them no he was straight. I asked why they thought that and they said look at the way he's dressed. I started laughing harder. I had been giving John a hard time already about his attire (clogs and a turtleneck, and possibly some glasses—I can't quite remember that detail). Later that day when I told John he thought it was hilarious, too.

We ended up befriending these women and their teammates from Barre, Vermont which led to some late-night drinking and a stupid human trick by one of the women. The trick—"butt darts." It's not as salacious as it sounds.

John taped it and it wasn't until recently that I finally found the tape. I am so happy that I did. The trick was accomplished by sticking a few dollars' worth of quarters into her ass crack (she was wearing pants) and then with her butt-cheeks clenched, waddling over to a cup on the ground and dropping them all into the cup. Sounds stupid, and it was, but it was also absolutely hilarious. Good times.

~ Todd 'Sarge' Kerrisey

It's really hard to be asked to tell my best JPM story.

The truth is, the stories blend together, each one better than the last, because we somehow always figured out a way to keep the fun living on in this continuous spectrum. That's where the name "Funbunch" ultimately came from in describing our small group of hockey-loving, hockey-covering crew.

I used to think of JPM and I much like a d-pair: that invisible ten-foot string always connecting us as we moved in sync through our work days.

We were creative collaborators, teammates, confidantes, family, driving buddies, bodyguards, therapists, wingmen, and yep, d-partners.

We were always aware of each other's whereabouts, what we each needed to accomplish, what moods we were in, and whether we had enough food and coffee to fuel us for that day (no one wants to work with hangry or decaffeinated togs/reporters).

Our texts started to become just one-word, because we could communicate with each other so seamlessly: "lobby" (I'm waiting for you in the hotel lobby so we can grab a cab together to get to the rink); "coach" (the coach is here for his morning interviews with the press, so grab the mic and get to the scrum NOW); "bux?" (want me to pick up a coffee for you at Starbucks?).

What I can tell you are about snippets of moments in time that stand out—like when he made Gordie Howe's statue come alive while I did a standup. Or how he turned a hotel's waiting area in Detroit into a living room for an interview. Or how we skated together at Fenway Park the very first time we saw it turn into an ice rink for the Winter Classic. How we stood in the middle of the picturesque, dark lit streets of Prague shooting a standup in literally the middle of the night.

Then there was the time on my very first preseason training trip with the Bruins. JPM saw Johnny Bucyk, said we should go over and say hi, and we ended up having a beer with the legend. A beer with Chief! What!!!

Most of what makes the highlight reel in my memory bank are the times JPM made everyone around him smile and relax, become comfortable around the gigantic camera he carried on his right shoulder, and just engage in simple, friendly, human conversation. You'd be surprised how hard that is to come by in this line of work.

If I really, really had to pick one story, it takes place in Nashville—the city that apparently also never sleeps.

We got into Nashville after a game, which meant we were flying in and getting to the hotel close to midnight. When you've been on the road night after night, and you're in different cities, and living out of a suitcase, you absolutely forget to appreciate where you are.

It was my first time in Nashville, but I didn't care, I was exhausted and just wanted to sleep. As always, we arrived and trudged through the hockey-player-filled hotel lobby with our suitcases, headed up to our respective rooms.

Then my phone rang. It was JPM, and I figured he wanted to plan out the next day before we called it a night.

JPM: "Let's go out. Just a quick walk."

Me: "I'm so freaking tired, I don't think I can."

JPM: "I'm tired, too, but we *have* to see Nashville. Ten minutes."

Famous last words. Our ten-minute walk turned into a two-hour tour of Nashville's hopping downtown.

We stopped at different bars to listen to various renditions of country music—hip hop-country, pop-country, punk-country, country-country. The city was blindingly alive, the music pushing time to a mere afterthought.

I remember saying when we finally got back to really call it a night—I'm so glad we did that. Because even though I could barely stay awake on double expresso at morning skate the next day, when would we ever see Nashville like this, in all its truthful glory, ever again?

The funny thing is, when I look back at all the photos we've taken through the years (mostly selfies, as he is the original selfie master), of all those times we spent working together, they're strikingly similar. Not the part where we're roaming the streets at night. But the part where we're just hysterically laughing.

Constantly meeting new people. Poking fun at ourselves. Walking the fine line between being professionals in suit jackets making television, and goof balling the heck out of life off-camera.

And that right there?

That's my JPM story.

~Naoko Funayama

As NESN's feature producer, you get teamed up with an ENG photographer. All four are more than capable. All have won various awards for their skill. When you have John Phillip Martin, aka JPM, as the photog for the day, well, your day is going to be an adventure.

Either a day spent at Hadlock Field in Portland, Maine or the Hockey Hall of Fame in Toronto, Ontario, JPM embraced each assignment with total enthusiasm. We have spent a lot of time together at many of the Red Sox minor league fields across the country.

Trips delivered us to Lancaster, California to Salem, Virginia to Pawtucket, Rhode Island. Each time, he shared with me his creative strategy, he plotted and asked questions about who we were going to interview. You see, JPM was just not a photog, but a producer as well. He thought and listened like one. Then, followed the interviews with shooting video to match their words.

We have covered over one hundred Red Sox prospects from Dustin Pedroia to Xander Bogaerts, and just about everybody in between. There was a lot of them who never made it to Fenway, but John's passion to tell the next prospect's story through his video he shot never wavered.

You can understand why when I was assigned a big project, I would always request JPM. It was not that the other NESN photogs couldn't do the work, it was that JPM and I had this connection. We always had a similar vision, not the same, but similar, meaning we would work out the differences.

One of those projects was the show *Jim Rice: Road to Cooperstown*. My goal was to tell Jim's journey from the segregated South to Fenway with his words and his friends from his hometown of Anderson, South Carolina. Something that has never been recorded before. Jim is an intensely private person, so when he agreed to the idea my first phone call was to JPM. You see, John already weighed in on the assignment, if it happens I am your guy.

On our drive to meet Jim at his home on our first day in Anderson, South Carolina, we developed our strategy, our combined vision. We pulled into Jim's driveway, and he is already in his vehicle waiting for us, and he is motioning to us to get in . . . NOW. We try to explain that we need to get the gear, but he waved that off, get in the car.

Jim proceeds to show us every field he ever played on—from football to track to baseball. As incredible as the tour was, we were NOT capturing it on tape. I looked back at John, sitting in the backseat, and we both had that same feeling, "we are missing the moment!!"

We started to explain to Jim how we needed our television gear, so we can record this tour. His answer still personifies the true Jim, he said, we can do it again tomorrow, just wanted to give you a preview.

Able to relax, John and I took in the tour and listened to Jim's incredible journey. Now armed with more info and what to shoot, John was determined to shoot every interview and B-roll in a unique fashion.

One that stands out, Jim explains to us that in his senior year of high school he was sent to the new "white" high school. We had Jim standing on his former street explaining how the town re-drew the lines that literally went down his street and through his house, forcing him to change schools. When I asked a follow-up question, about through not around his house, Jim replied, my sister was a sophomore, they didn't take her, just me.

John captured more than Jim's words, he captured his reflective thought moments after those words. Something John did throughout our time with Jim in his hometown. John instinctively knew to keep the camera on Jim, we can get B-roll later, the story was Jim.

This was a story of a proud man, who was proud of his journey from the segregated South to Cooperstown. John captured Jim's persona throughout numerous interviews during our time together. This was JPM at his best, camera on his shoulder, feeling the moment, zooming in or pulling out, to capture the mood of the subject.

~Steve Garabedian

I've been with NESN since January 2000. Initially, I worked on studio-based shows and John and the other photogs were often traveling to shoot features and show segments, which means I knew John only in passing. After becoming a member of the remote production crews for the Red Sox and Bruins, I would mostly be offsite. A couple of years later, the staff photographers began to accompany our Red Sox and Bruins production crews on a rotating basis. This meant that the seat next to me on the team charter for road trips would be occupied by our ENG photographer. This is when I came to know JPM. He taught me useful things like how best to distribute salt onto a meal—pour it in one hand, clap your hands together over your food and then rub both hands together. Perfect. (For some reason, pepper was never given such a special presentation, but simply sprinkled onto food straight out of the shaker.) It was a ritual we repeated many, many times over the years. John also caused me to never use my headphones. They would be ready around my neck, but John and I would chat it up from takeoff to touch down. JPM and I would get into it about everything. I miss him on every flight since his last.

Anyway, given that I sat with all the NESN photogs on a rotating basis for travel to and from road games—with each of them bringing something to the table—it's ironic that one of the best memories of John that sticks out in my mind is a trip from Montreal back to Massachusetts by car.

It was 2011 and the Bruins had lost to the Canadiens in Game Six of the first round of the playoffs, evening the series at three games apiece. For whatever reason, Game Seven was scheduled for the next night back in Boston, a game from which many of us now can picture Nathan Horton scoring in overtime to propel the Bruins to the second round of the playoffs and eventually their 2011 Stanley Cup.

John and I had decided before the game that if a Game Seven became reality, we would drive back to Massachusetts overnight in an effort to get home as soon as possible. The trip takes five hours or so and a benefit of driving overnight would mean there would be no traffic. I had done the drive several times over the years. With John at the wheel, we left Montreal around 11 p.m. with an estimated arrival in our neighboring towns around 4 a.m. We made it most of the way to the U.S. Border with threatening skies but no real rain.

Upon entering the United States, the skies opened up. This was the kind of rain I've rarely, if ever, seen. Ridiculously heavy rain is a ridiculous understatement. For anyone that's ever driven from Montreal to the Boston Area, you go through some pretty nice mountains in Vermont. We were doing this at night, alone on the road with just buckets and buckets of rain coming down and crazy intense lightning all over. John was unaffected. He was cruising through this mountainous terrain, on unfamiliar and winding stretches of road, in a pitch-black deluge with frequent bolts everywhere. I was white-knuckled for the remainder of the trip. John had one hand on the steering wheel of the sedan I had rented, cruising along at sixty-five miles an hour as though it were a sunny day.

Luckily for me, I had John to keep my mind off the fact that at any moment we would be Thelma & Louise-ing off a cliff, sliding off the road and into a forest or encountering a moose with visibility nil.

John was cool as a cucumber. Nothing specific in our conversation from that night has stayed with me, though I guarantee that there were no lulls of silence. We survived and thanks to John, we thrived. JPM is an everyman, but so extraordinarily disarming, charming, personable and HILARIOUS that he is completely unique.

These qualities and more made JPM an awesome seat-mate on planes, trains, and automobiles all over North America. They make him an awesome friend to go with to grab a beer, a coffee, a meal and maybe another beer or two. For all the important and inane conversations we had while above the clouds, for every perfectly salted meal we enjoyed—these memories are for you JPM.

~Patrick White

The best time of the year for the photogs was playoffs, especially hockey. Most of the year when you traveled it was one photog at a time. There were four of us at NESN, and we were a very close-knit group, not because we hung out all the time, but because we were the only guys that knew what each other was going through. The schedule was crazy, the travel was nonstop, and as I said before you spent a lot of time separate from the rest of the crew. It's just an odd job that doesn't make sense sometimes. Only another photog really gets the oddity of the schedule and the travel.

During the playoffs, things changed. The workload doubled. More media, more press conferences, more shots needed for pre and postgame shows. NESN would travel two photogs. Traveling in the playoffs was fun! It's like an adult sleepover.

We were all close to the crews from all the travel, but now we got to add a close friend to the trips! Imagine if your boss came up to you and said, "Hey, I'm thinking the next three months you should bring your best friend to work." That's how it felt to us.

Don't get me wrong we busted our butts, but it didn't feel like work 'cause you were doing it with a close friend that hadn't been by your side in a year or so. In 2011 John and I were picked to do the Philly series during the Bruins Stanley Cup playoff run. This was coming after an amazing week of hijinks in Montreal. John had traveled for one game, and it was out of this world fun, but Philly was where we cemented our nickname for the next half dozen years. Like most people who travel for work, we would do our best to get out of the hotel at night. We would get the job done to the best of our ability, and then go out for drinks as a crew—to the best of our ability! Our group was starting to get a reputation as always horsing around, being a little too loud, and borderline not taking the work seriously . . . we were of course, taking every second of the job serious, but we had a great way of knowing that these moments don't happen often, so you have to enjoy it too!

I always tell people that the 2011 Stanley Cup run probably took a few years off the back end of my life! I don't think I missed going out more than one or two nights!

John was king of making sure we made everything fun. He would be the guy pushing to finish the job and get up to the press box so we didn't miss the anthem. He would be the guy to say we had to go take a picture with the ice girls because we could. He was the guy always pushing the fact that we may not get here again. Making sure we took pictures and had memories of the trip documented. He was taking selfies with a little Blackberry camera (original selfie king). The guy was a trendsetter when it came to having fun!

In the bowels of the arena, most of the media would pile into one or two rooms to do everything. Writers would write, videographers would store their gear, reporters would do stand-ups, and live-shots, and producers would make phone calls. It was always a little chaotic because there was so much going on in one room. We were the group that annoyed everyone! We were always laughing and having a good time. I know that doesn't seem annoying on the surface, but when you're trying to write an article and make a deadline . . . my cackle is the last thing you want in your life.

We're down in this room after morning skate of Game Two in Philly, and we're doing our usual horsing around when you hear from the writers' corner, "God, do they ever stop?" There was silence. No one spoke for a good ten seconds, which feels like an eternity when the insult is hurled at you.

Then a dry voice rose up. "You mean the Funbunch?"

Another second or two went by and John started howling, he shouted back, "Hey, we're the Funbunch!"

We didn't have a name before that, but from that moment on, we wore that moniker with pride. We indeed were the Funbunch. The nickname lasted for years!

I even recall Andy Brickly talking to someone about the transition from being a pro athlete to being a commentator. He said "it's different teams, but we still treat each other like we're on a team. I used to be on the Bruins, now I'm on the Funbunch."

John Martin set the tone for Funbunching, and we all ran with it.

Almost literally later that day, we decided after the game due to a very short turnaround we should tailgate outside the arena rather than go to a bar. If you're not from Pennsylvania, it can be a daunting task to get a case of beer. Beer is sold at bars. You can go to your local pub or restaurant to get a six pack, but if you want more than that you have to go to a state-run store. Finding one is not easy.

We spent the time between morning skate, and pregame stuff (a couple hours) looking for where to get a case of beer. We finally discovered there was a store across town, and we had just enough time to get there. Even if we didn't have time, we were going anyway!

The store looked more like a three-bay mechanic shop. It was massive, concrete, cold, and filled with beer. John walked in, grabbed a cold thirty rack of Bud Light, marched to the front desk, and asked if they had ice, and a Styrofoam cooler. The guy at the front said he had ice, but no coolers. Before he could even suggest where to go and get a cooler, John started spitballing ideas of how to keep the beer cold. If John were the leader of an Army figuring out how to storm the fortress, I would have run through the moat, smashed my face through the brick wall, slain the dragon, saved the princess, and stolen the kingdom all by myself, just to keep the beer cold. You could see the guy working the beer store felt the same way!

"Sir, we need your help. We are in dire need of keeping these beers cold for a few hours, and you have no coolers. Do you have trash bags?"

The beer store guy jumped up from his chair and grabbed two or three trash bags. (Amazing how I can't remember how many trash bags, but I can remember every word of John's epic speech).

The wheels were in full motion, and the beer store guy excitedly said, "I can get you a big cardboard box, and you can line it with the trash bags!"

We were giddy with excitement as to how this whole thing was coming together. As the beer store guy ran through the garage like store to the back looking for a cardboard box, John walked into the middle of the store and started yelling as if he were some sort of movie president giving a speech to the country before it came under attack from aliens . . ."This, this right here is what I love about America . . . People, good people, helping people . . . to get drunk."

I slow clapped.

That was John Martin. Taking a moment that just should have been about grabbing a case of beer and turning into a triumphant moment of joy between strangers . . . people helping people . . . to get drunk.

~Bryan Brennan

THE RAINBOW INCIDENT

Spring of 2002, my second Fort Myers spring training.

A long six weeks spent traveling across Florida. I only did around eight games a spring on TV so daily *Sports Desk* reports were filed after each game. Basically, a news of the day report with a stand up after each game with that day's stadium as a backdrop. Then later that night we would send the tape back to Boston via WINK TV.

John and I were close friends but after four weeks of traveling daily in a hot and smelly rental van across Florida our patience for each other was waning.

This one particular day it was raining in Fort Myers and I was sure that we did not need to make the two and a half hour trip to Fort Lauderdale for a day game and would be off, only to find out a producer thought otherwise that we still needed to go to do a stand up at the stadium, even if it was rained out.

Miserable. Off we went. John Martin was a photojournalist first, but truth be known he saw himself as an artist and his canvas was on the other side of the lens.

We arrived in Fort Lauderdale and had a two-hour rain delay then the game was played. After five and a half hours, the game ends and we do our report with an opening shot of me on the field and then close the report with a stand up in front of the stadium entrance. Making it very clear we were there.

We are done. Time to drive back to Fort Myers now with traffic in the Miami area. I am in and out of sleep, raging headache.

All of a sudden, back on the West Coast side on I-75 John sees a "rainbow." He always assumed driving responsibilities and slammed on the brakes as if we were going to hit something, jarring me awake and while in the fast lane pulled left three lanes over to the shoulder. He jumps out of the van and runs to the back to pull out his tripod and camera. Only he forgot to put the van in park. John jumps back in the driver side, slams on the brakes and puts it in park. Looks at me, and I am visibly upset but unable to speak. Out he goes again.

I look back as he sets up his camera. He gets the shot and goes up and down the rainbow slowly from one end to the other then zooms in and out quickly and then in slow motion.

Ten minutes pass, my heart rate has calmed and he gets back in the van and is silent for about ten minutes.

He then says in a quiet and calm tone, "You know how mad you were when we headed back into traffic in the van? You are really going to be upset now! I just realized that in taping the rainbow I taped over and erased your stand up from Fort Lauderdale."

There were no words. Not at that moment.

We had to reshoot my standup somewhere in Fort Myers before the tape feed later that evening.

We did not speak for an hour and then I remember exactly what I said.

"John, where was the rainbow going to air, F-ing Sportsdesk?"

~Don Orsillo

ABOUT THE AUTHOR

~JPM~

1 TIME HUBBY

2 TIME DAD

1979 BEST BACK-PAXTON PANTHERS FOOTBALL

2007 SOUTH END BASEBALL-HALL OF FAME

2010 SOUTH END BASEBALL CHAMPS-ANGELS

5 TIME BOSTON/NEW ENGLAND EMMY AWARD WINNER

30 YEARS SOUTHEND BASEBALL-ANGELS COACH

113 GRATEFUL DEAD SHOWS

60 BOB DYLAN SHOWS

SOON TO BE BESTSELLING AUTHOR

ACKNOWLEDGEMENTS

Adrienne, Kaia and Gabby Martin, Camille Martin (Mom), Denise and Don Hein, Susan Martin, Jim Martin, Linda Asta, Bruce Embry, Andrea Celenza, Owen Carlson, Patrick Gamere, Chris DelDotto, Bryan Brennan, Eric Scharmer, Steve Garabedian, Nancy J. Rose, Chris Larson, Heather Barraclough, Dan Brokowski, Rob Kirwan, Doug Rose, Michael and Carolyn Crowley, Pete and Norine Shults, Clay DeBrew, Coco and Rusty Young, Susi Prescott, Christine Borgford, Jumba Grace, Ssekilime Hudson, Tony and Katie Saia

Made in the USA
Columbia, SC
16 November 2019